the Master Teacher Series

Reading Comprehension

For the master teachers who allowed me to study and film their instruction.

Published by The Teaching Doctors

 To order additional copies of this book or schedule workshops for teachers, contact

http://www.teachingdoctors.com
schacter@teachingdoctors.com

The Teaching Doctors
22 Pearce Mitchell Place
Stanford, CA 94305

Schacter, John
ISBN 0-9770954-2-8

the Master Teacher Series

Reading Comprehension

Contents

The Master Teacher Series: Reading Comprehension

This book and DVD series weaves the best in educational research with practical examples that show the theory in action. In this volume, we present over 30 scientifically proven reading comprehension strategies that increase student achievement from 15 to 100 percent. Each strategy is explained step-by-step and through visual lesson storyboards. Half of the strategies are accompanied by videos of master teachers demonstrating them in their classrooms.

Writing this book and providing the video teaching examples would not have been possible without the master teachers who contributed their time and opened their classrooms. Thank you Toni Greene, Suzie Throop, Nikki Serafin, Karen Wild, Suzanna Llamas, Lynn Alloway, Debbie Gordon, Bonnie Price, Maricela Sandoval, Tess Weisbarth, Andy de Seriere, Beth Higgins, Charmon Evans, and Judy Crenshaw. Appreciation is also expressed to Tom Magallanes for his artistic graphic design and Katharine Fry for her editorial feedback and copyediting.

Teachers Learning Together

We think this book and DVDs will work best when used by groups of teachers. Reading, discussing, viewing and revising these strategies may help teachers refine their practices to meet their students diverse learning needs.

Book Overview

In the prologue, we describe United States elementary and middle school students' reading achievement. Chapters 1 through 7 introduce over 30 research-based reading comprehension strategies that significantly increase students' recall of ideas, ability to draw conclusions, make inferences, and solve problems. Chapter 8 discusses the research on expert readers and suggests how to use this research to improve comprehension instruction.

We have provided a wide variety of proven reading comprehension strategies to appeal to both new and veteran teachers. It is our hope that all teachers will try several of these approaches to expand their instructional repertoire and increase their students' understanding of what they read.

Reading Comprehension Instruction

In 2005, a countrywide sample of fourth- and eighth-grade American students took the National Assessment of Educational Progress (NAEP). The reading portion of the test required pupils to interpret literary materials, informational texts, and practical manuscripts (e.g., bus and train schedules, directions, forms, etc.).

It turned out that after spending five hours reading and answering questions, only 30 percent of fourth- and eighth-grade students "showed an overall understanding of the information they read." Close to 70 percent could not "make clear inferences, draw conclusions, or connect what they read to their own experiences."

As a former elementary school teacher, I wanted a little more information about how the National Assessment measured reading comprehension. So I obtained several of the test's texts and comprehension questions. Below is a poem eighth-grade students read.

The Fish

I caught a tremendous fish
and held him beside the boat
half out of water, with my hook
fast in a corner of his mouth.
5 *He didn't fight.*
He hadn't fought at all.
He hung a grunting weight,
battered and venerable
and homely. Here and there
10 *his brown skin hung in strips*
like ancient wallpaper,
and its pattern of darker brown
was like wallpaper:
shapes like full-blown roses
15 *stained and lost through age.*
He was speckled with barnacles,
fine rosettes of lime,
and infested
with tiny white sea-lice,
20 *and underneath two or three*
rags of green weed hung down.
While his gills were breathing in
the terrible oxygen
—the frightening gills,
25 *fresh and crisp with blood,*
that can cut so badly—
I thought of the coarse white flesh
packed in like feathers,
the big bones and the little bones,
30 *the dramatic reds and blacks*
of his shiny entrails,
and the pink swim-bladder
like a big peony.
I looked into his eyes
35 *which were far larger than mine*
but shallower, and yellowed,
the irises backed and packed
with tarnished tinfoil
seen through the lenses
40 *of old scratched isinglass.*
They shifted a little, but not
to return my stare.
It was more like the tipping
of an object toward the light.
45 *I admired his sullen face,*
the mechanism of his jaw,
and then I saw
that from his lower lip
if you could call it a lip
50 *grim, wet, and weaponlike,*
hung five old pieces of fish-line,
or four and a wire leader
with the swivel still attached,
with all their five big hooks
55 *grown firmly in his mouth.*
A green line, frayed at the end
where he broke it, two heavier lines,
and a fine black thread
still crimped from the strain and snap
60 *when it broke and he got away.*
Like medals with their ribbons
frayed and wavering,
a five-haired beard of wisdom
trailing from his aching jaw.
65 *I stared and stared*
and victory filled up
the little rented boat,
from the pool of bilge
where oil had spread a rainbow
70 *around the rusted engine*
to the bailer rusted orange,
the sun-cracked thwarts,
the oarlocks on their strings,
the gunnels—until everything
75 *was rainbow, rainbow, rainbow!*
And I let the fish go.

After students read this poem, the National Assessment asked them to answer the questions below.

"Why does the person let the fish go? What in the poem makes you think so?"

Only 30% of eighth graders wrote a response that demonstrated they could make and support such an inference.

"Reread the lines beginning with "I admired" (line 45) and ending with "aching jaw" (line 64). What do these lines tell you about the fish's experience?"

Only 29% of students could draw correct conclusions about the fish's experience.

"Explain how the language used in this poem is different from the language used in everyday speech."

Only 26% of students answered this question correctly.

What's interesting about these eighth graders' test scores in 2005 is that they are virtually identical to their test scores in 2000. In fact, for close to 30 years, only 30 percent of American students have achieved proficiency in reading (see *NAEP Percent Proficient in Reading* chart on the next page).

Why Can't Students Understand What They Read?

During the reading wars, researchers and policymakers argued that students could not understand what they read because they lacked the decoding and sight word skills necessary to read fluently. However, as the Early Childhood Longitudinal Study demonstrates, today's kindergarten to third grade students made large improvements in decoding, sight word recognition, and understanding words in context (all components of fluent reading).

The one area, though, where student achievement continued to lag behind was interpreting text. Much like their fourth-grade and eighth-grade counterparts, only 30 percent of third graders can proficiently comprehend what they read.

Early Childhood Longitudinal Study
Percent Demonstrating Proficiency

	Kindergarten	First Grade	Third Grade
Identifying Sounds	54	94	100
Sight Word Recognition	14	83	95
Understanding Words in Context	4	48	99
Interpreting Text	n/a	n/a	29

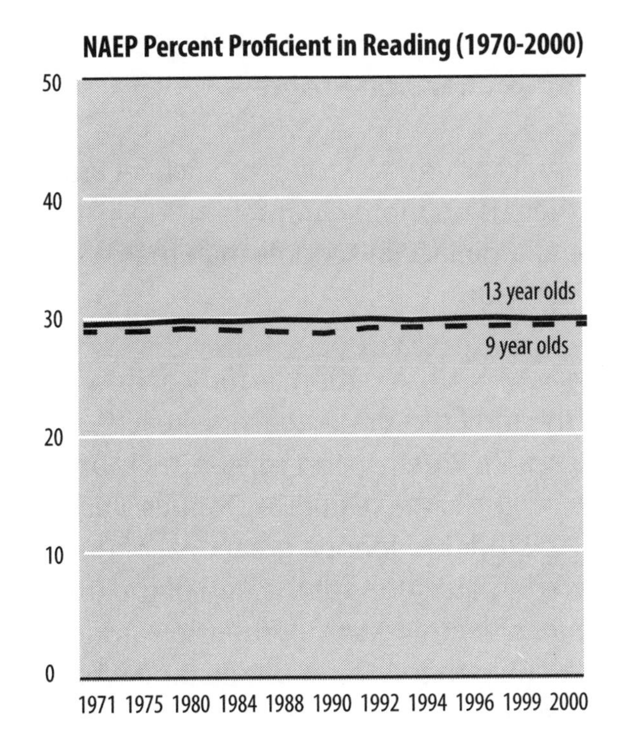

Time Spent Teaching Comprehension

Thirty years ago, a researcher named Dolores Durkin conducted a study where she measured comprehension strategy instruction in upper-elementary grade classrooms. After roughly 4,500 minutes of observation, Durkin documented only 20 minutes of reading comprehension instruction. She noted that teachers spent almost all of their time asking students questions, but little time teaching students strategies for how to answer them.

On the basis of these results, reading researchers set out to improve comprehension instruction. First, they studied what highly capable readers thought and did while they read. These scholars discovered that expert readers were extremely active. Before reading, they have a purpose, goal, and plan. They activate what they know about the subject to make connections and predictions about what they are going to read.

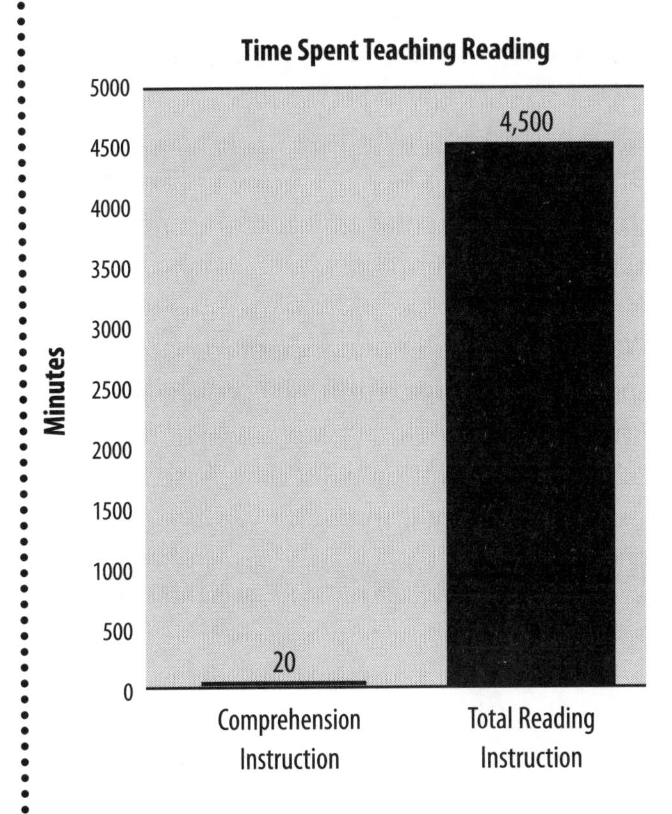

During reading, proficient readers develop hypotheses and draw conclusions. They fill in information gaps, react to the text emotionally, and relate ideas to one another. Capable readers also make inferences, ask questions, and monitor their attention.

After reading, experts continue to process the text. They do so by writing summaries, answering questions, and even re-reading and rehearsing information they want to remember.

This research on expert readers led to the development of comprehension strategies for students. Not surprisingly, when students were taught comprehension strategies, their understanding, recall, and ability to make inferences dramatically increased. More specifically, when students were taught and applied these expert comprehension strategies to a variety of texts, their reading achievement scores increased 15 to 100 percent.

Yet despite the abundance of research and proliferation of scientifically proven reading comprehension strategies over the last 20 years, the National Reading Assessment scores have not improved. Why?

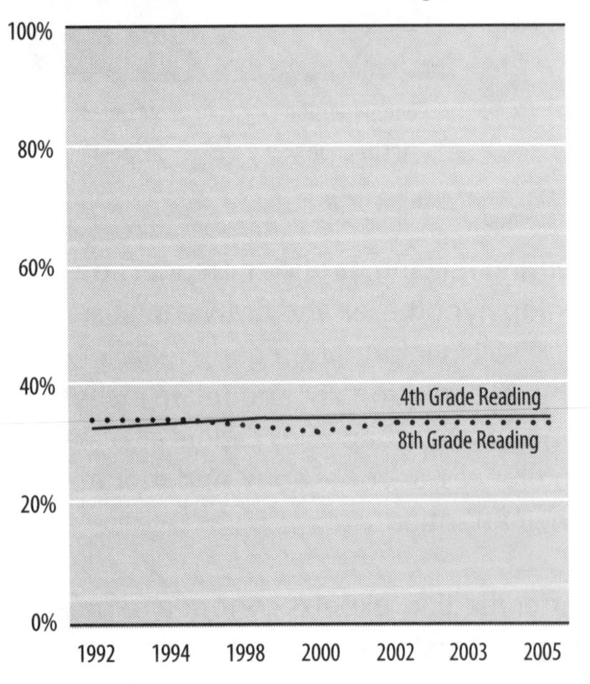

An Explanation for the Lack of Comprehension Progress

Today, according to Professor Michael Pressley, there is no more comprehension instruction taking place in schools than there was 30 years ago.

In his recent observational study of how fourth- and fifth- grade teachers teach reading, Dr. Pressley and colleagues found virtually the same results as Dolores Durkin. That is, students spent a great deal of time answering questions at the end of the text instead of learning comprehension strategies to help them better understand what they read.

What is clear from the last 30 years of reading comprehension research is:

1. There are a number of scientifically proven comprehension strategies that increase student reading achievement.
2. These comprehension strategies are not finding their way into classrooms.

The purpose of this book is to share these strategies with teachers so that they can use them to increase their students understanding of what they read.

References

Bishop, E. (1979). *The Fish*. In the Complete Poems1927-1979 by Elizabeth Bishop. Reprinted by permission of Farrar, Straus and Giroux.

Durkin, D. (1978-79). What classroom observations reveal about reading comprehension instruction. *Reading Research Quarterly, 15*, 481-533.

Haller, E. R, Child, D. A., & Walberg, H. J. (1988). Can comprehension be taught? A quantitative synthesis of "metacognitive" studies. *Educational Researcher, 17*, 5-8.

National Center for Education Statistics (2004). *From kindergarten through third grade: Children's beginning school experiences*. Institute for Educational Sciences, United States Department of Education, Washington, DC.

Pressley, M. & Wharton-McDonald, R. (1997). Skilled comprehension and its development through instruction. *School Psychology Review, 26*, 279-304.

Pressley, M., Wharton-McDonald, R, Mistretta, J., & Echevarria, M. (1998). *The nature of literacy instruction in ten grade 4/5 classrooms in upstate New York. Elementary School Journal, 99*, 101-128.

U.S. Department of Education (2005). *The nation's report card: Reading 2005*. National Center for Education Statistics, Washington, DC.

Wyatt, D., Pressley, M., El-Dinery, P., Stein, S., Evans, P., & Brown, R. (1993). Comprehension strategies, worth and credibility monitoring, and evaluations: Cold and hot cognition when experts read professional articles that are important to them. *Learning and Individual Differences, 5*, 49-72.

Questioning

1

1 Definition

Socrates showed that with careful, successive questioning, learning is greatly enhanced. But who learns more? Those who ask questions, or answer them?

2 Chapter Preview

This chapter presents:

- Four question generation strategies with accompanying visual lesson storyboards.
- Three videos of master teachers instructing their students how to generate questions while they read.

3 Research

Experimental studies by Allison King and a review of the research by Barak Rosenshine demonstrate that when students are taught how to ask questions while they read, they perform 14 to 50 percent better on standardized comprehension tests. In addition, these students are more likely to pinpoint their misunderstandings, and develop sound inferences.

Notes

Question Cue Cards

STRATEGY 1:

Question Cue Cards

Question Cue Cards provide students with a variety of prompts that help them generate questions before, during, and after they read.

Step-by-Step

1. Teacher provides each student with a *Question Cue Card* (see storyboard #1).
2. Using an overhead projector, the teacher reads a short passage aloud (see storyboard #2).
   a. Teacher stops after reading one paragraph.
   b. She refers to her *Question Cue Card* and develops a question.
   c. Teacher asks question, thinks of and verbalizes an answer, and continues reading repeating the process.
3. After modeling how to use the *Question Cue Card*, the teacher practices with students by requiring them to read paragraphs on the overhead and use their *Question Cue Cards* to generate questions (see storyboards #4 and #5).
4. When students can proficiently use the *Cue Card*, the teacher distributes index cards to pairs.
5. Pairs are assigned to read, stop after each paragraph or two, then write their question on the front of the index card, and the answer on the back.
6. At the end of the passage, pairs have several questions and answers written on index cards.
7. The teacher assigns pairs to pass their stack of index card questions to another pair who reads and answers them. Pairs answer two stacks of questions before the end of the lesson (see storyboards #6 and #7).

1

Today we are going to use a comprehension strategy called *Question Cue Cards* to help us better understand the circulatory system. Every pair of students will get a *Question Cue Card* along with a stack of index cards. As you read, you'll stop after each paragraph and use the *Question Cue Card* to generate a question. You'll then write that question on the front of an index card, and write the answer on the back.

QUESTION CUE CARD

1. Describe ________in your own words.
2. What does _______ mean?
3. Why is ________ important?
4. How is _____ related to _____?
5. Explain how ________.
6. How are _____ and ______ similar?
7. What's different between______and _____?
8. What causes ______?
9. What would happen if _______?

2

I'm going to read the first paragraph from our article. Watch how I stop at the end of the paragraph and use the *Question Cue Card* to help me generate questions.

Circulatory System

The circulatory system in humans is composed of the heart and blood vessels—arteries, veins, and capillaries. Its purpose is to provide nutrients and oxygen to the tissues, and to remove wastes from them. It is also where the body fights infections.

QUESTION CUE CARD

1. Describe ___________ in your own words.
2. What does ___________ mean?
3. Why is ___________ important?
4. How is ______ related to ________?
5. Explain how ___________.
6. How are ______ and ______ similar?
7. What's different between_____ and _____?
8. What causes _________?
9. What would happen if ___________?

Teacher Question
Describe the purpose of the circulatory system in your own words?

Question Cue Cards

3

Now I'll read the next paragraph and use my Cue Card to write two more questions.

Circulatory System

The circulatory system can be considered as composed of two parts: the systemic circulation, which serves the body as a whole except for the lungs, and the pulmonary circulation, which carries the blood to and from the lungs. The organs of the circulatory system consist of vessels that carry the blood and a muscular pump, the heart, that drives the blood.

QUESTION CUE CARD

1. Describe ________ in your own words.
2. What does ________ mean?
3. Why is ________ important?
4. How is _____ related to _______?
5. Explain how ________.
6. How are _____ and _____ similar?
7. What's different between____ and ____?
8. What causes ________?
9. What would happen if ________?

Teacher Question
What's different between systemic circulation and pulmonary circulation?

Teacher Question
What would happen if you didn't have organs?

4

Notice how I'm using the *Question Cue Card* to help me ask questions while I read? Let's have you practice this strategy with a partner. I'm putting the next paragraph about the circulatory system on the overhead. Read it and use the *Cue Card* to write a question.

Circulatory System

Of the vessels, the arteries carry blood away from the heart; the main artrial vessel, the aorta, branches into smaller arteries, which in turn branch into still smaller vessels and reach all parts of the body. Within the body tissues, the vessels are microscopic capillaries through which gas and nutrient exchange occurs. Blood leaving the tissue capillaries enters converging vessels, the veins, to return to the heart and lungs.

QUESTION CUE CARD

1. Describe ________ in your own words.
2. What does ________ mean?
3. Why is ________ important?
4. How is _____ related to _______?
5. Explain how ________.
6. How are _____ and _____ similar?
7. What's different between____ and ____?
8. What causes ________?
9. What would happen if ________?

Student Question
Why is the aorta artery important?

Student Question
How are arteries and veins similar?

Student Question
What does capillaries mean?

5

Excellent questions. Let's practice with another two paragraphs.

Circulatory System

The right atrium of the heart is the larger of the two atriums because it needs to hold the larger amount of blood coming from the body (as opposed to the blood coming from the lungs). The deoxygenated blood leaves the heart by the pulmonary arteries and travels through the lungs (where it is oxygenated).

The oxygenated blood then enters the left atrium of the heart, where blood is pumped into the aorta artery and is carried throughout the body.

QUESTION CUE CARD

1. Describe ________ in your own words.
2. What does ________ mean?
3. Why is ________ important?
4. How is _____ related to _______?
5. Explain how ________.
6. How are _____ and _____ similar?
7. What's different between____ and ____?
8. What causes ________?
9. What would happen if ________?

Student Question
What's different between the right and left atrium?

Student Question
Explain how deoxygenated blood travels through the body.

6

You generated some great questions. When you go back to your seats you'll have a stack of index cards (▭), your *Question Cue Card* (■), and the article about the circulatory system (□). With a partner (●●), your job is to read the article and to write three questions and answers on your index cards after each page.

TEACHER DESK

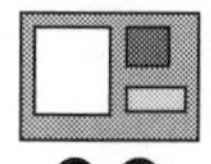
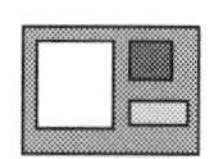
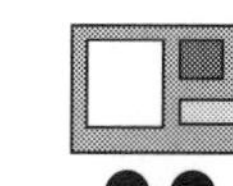
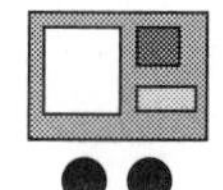
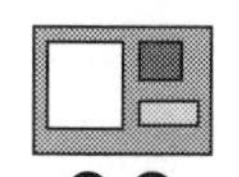
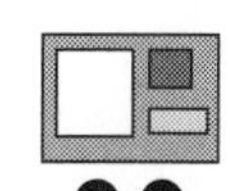

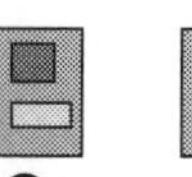
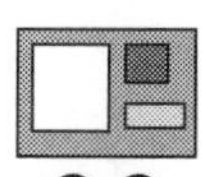
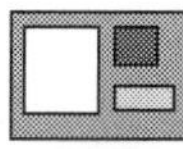
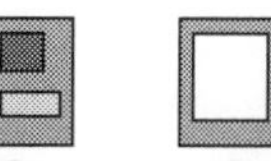

Question Cue Cards

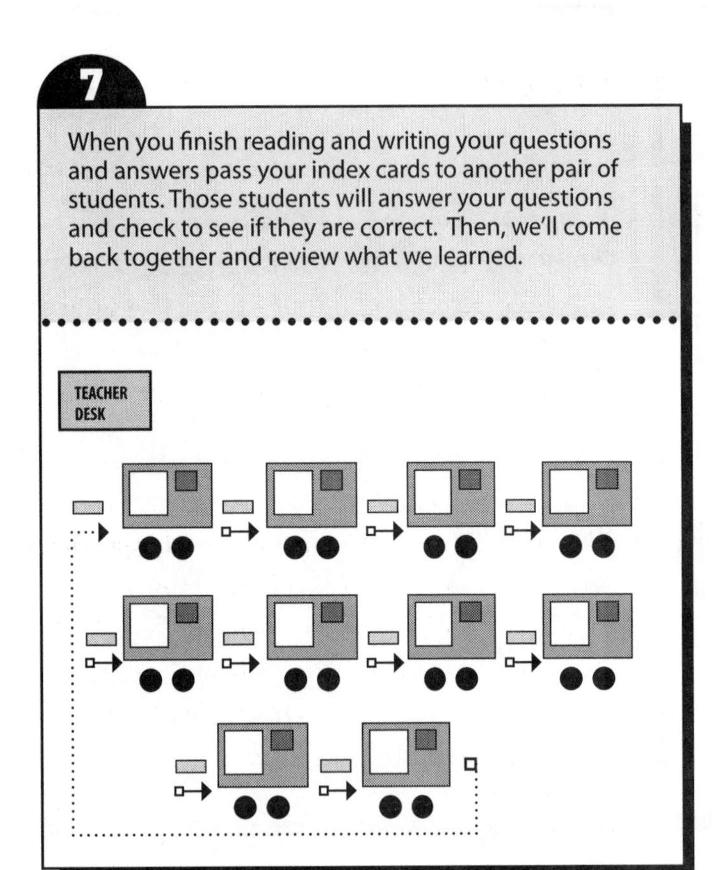

STRATEGY 2:

Developing Thin & Thick Questions

When students are taught to generate their own questions, they invariably start by writing factual questions that require answers drawn directly from the text. Generating factual questions increases recall, but it does little to develop more advanced reading comprehension skills like making inferences, drawing conclusions, or connecting the text with one's personal experience. Teaching students to convert **thin** (factual) questions, into **thick** (inferential) questions is a valuable skill.

Step-by-Step

1. Teacher introduces the idea that there are two types of questions: **thin** (factual) and **thick** (inferential). Teacher describes **thin** questions as ones whose answers can be found in the text. She explains that to answer **thick** questions, readers have to think to come up with an answer and use the text to support it.
2. Teacher draws a T-chart with columns labeled **thin** and **thick**. She writes a sample **thin** question for a book the class has just completed (see storyboard #2).
3. Teacher asks students to come up with more **thin** questions. After listing several **thin** questions, the teacher encourages students to answer them.
4. Next, the teacher changes a **thin** question into a **thick** one. As she answers the thick question, she shows how her response uses her knowledge and the text for support (see storyboard #3).
5. Teacher encourages students to look at the list of **thin** questions and change two into **thick** questions on their own. She provides students with **thick** question prompts, like *How, Why, Could,* or *Imagine.*
6. After students have practiced changing **thin** questions into **thick** questions, the teacher places a transparency of the first page of a new text students will read on the overhead. She reads the first two paragraphs aloud and writes a **thin** question. She asks students to each write a **thin** question (see storyboard #4).
7. Next, she instructs students to write a **thick** question (see storyboard #5).
8. The teacher repeats steps 6 and 7 for two more paragraphs.
9. Teacher assigns students to pairs, provides them with the text to read (preferably a short selection), and asks students to write three **thin** questions on one side of their T- chart and three **thick** questions on the other side (see storyboard #6).
10. Teacher closes the lesson with a review of the **thin** and **thick** questions students produced.

Developing Thin & Thick Questions

1

Most times when we read, we answer questions at the end of the text. Or, in our reading groups I'm the one asking all the questions. Well today, you are going to ask the questions. I'm going to draw a T-chart on the whiteboard and label one column *Thin* and the other *Thick*.

DEVELOPING THIN & THICK QUESTIONS

Thin	Thick

2

Thin questions have answers that you can find directly in the text. *Thick* questions make you think because the answer requires both your personal knowledge and the text details for support. Watch me think of and write two *thin* questions from the first three chapters of *Captain Underpants*.

DEVELOPING THIN & THICK QUESTIONS

Thin	Thick
What hero did George and Harold create and draw comics about?	
Which two things do George and Harold have in common?	

ANSWER Captain Underpants

ANSWER They are both in fourth grade and they both like practical jokes.

Can you find the answers for these two questions in the text? Sure you can.

3

How can we change a *thin* question so that you can't find the exact answer in the story, but you have to use the story and your own thinking to support your answer?

DEVELOPING THIN & THICK QUESTIONS

Thin	Thick
What hero did George and Harold create and draw comics about?	What makes Captain Underpants funny?
Which three things do George and Harold have in common?	Even though George and Harold get in a lot of trouble, the author says they both are good boys. Why?

Answer: Nothing in the story says what makes Captain Underpants funny. You have to think of how he looks, what he says, and what he does.

Answer: George and Harold get in trouble for pranks and their comic book, BUT they listen to their teachers, they don't intentionally try to hurt people, they are kind to their friends, and they work hard.

The story does not tell you why George and Harold are good boys. You have to analyze their actions and what they say and do to come up with and support your answer.

4

We read the first three chapters together. Now it's your turn to read chapters 4 through 6 in pairs. Your job is to write three *thin* questions on Post-it Notes. When you are finished, place those Post-its under the *Thin question* column in our T-chart.

DEVELOPING THIN & THICK QUESTIONS

Thin	Thick
Where did Harold and George hide?	
What pranks did George and Harold play at the football game?	
Which two children did Mr. Krupp hate most of all?	
Which threat made Harold and George do what Mr. Krupp said?	
What things did Mr. Krupp hate?	
Why did the football float away?	
Which punishment were Harold and George most afraid of?	
How did Principal Krupp catch Harold and George and what did he do?	

Developing Thin & Thick Questions

5

What great *thin* questions! Let's pick three of them and see if we can turn them into *thick* questions.

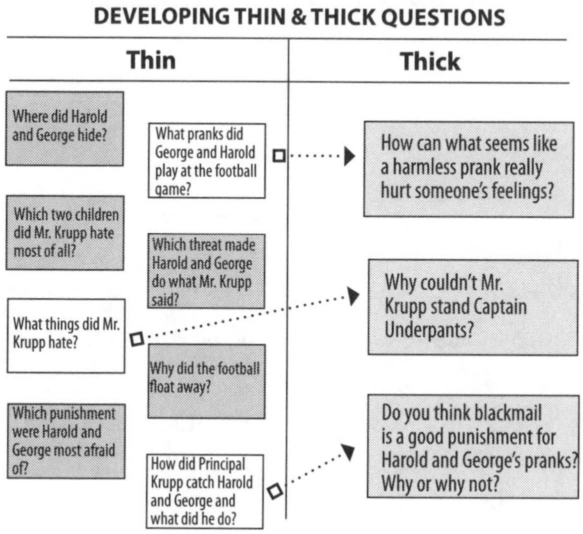

DEVELOPING THIN & THICK QUESTIONS

Thin	Thick
Where did Harold and George hide?	
What pranks did George and Harold play at the football game?	How can what seems like a harmless prank really hurt someone's feelings?
Which two children did Mr. Krupp hate most of all?	
Which threat made Harold and George do what Mr. Krupp said?	
What things did Mr. Krupp hate?	Why couldn't Mr. Krupp stand Captain Underpants?
Why did the football float away?	
Which punishment were Harold and George most afraid of?	
How did Principal Krupp catch Harold and George and what did he do?	Do you think blackmail is a good punishment for Harold and George's pranks? Why or why not?

6

Explain what makes these questions *thick* questions? How are they different from *thin* questions? Tomorrow we'll read three more chapters from *Captain Underpants,* and this time you'll have your own T-chart where you will write three *thin* and three *thick* questions of your own.

DEVELOPING THIN & THICK QUESTIONS

Thin	Thick

STRATEGY 3:

Who, What, Where, Why & How

This strategy makes use of question word stems to help students generate a wide variety of questions while they read. Then, through a cooperative learning structure called *Numbered Heads Together*, teams of students answer the questions they generate.

Step-by-Step

1. Teacher creates a poster with the question words *Who, What, Where, Why*, & *How* (see storyboard #2).
   a. She places a text selection on the overhead projector and reads the first paragraph aloud.
   b. Next, she consults her question words poster and says, "I'm going to ask a *Why* question." She verbalizes and then writes her *Why* question (see storyboard #3).
   c. Teacher reads another paragraph aloud, consults her chart again and says, "Let's see, I think I can ask a *Who* question." She verbalizes and writes her *Who* question (see storyboard #4).
   d. Teacher repeats the process a final time.
2. After modeling how to ask questions, the teacher assigns reading material to pairs of students who alternate roles between reading a paragraph aloud and thinking of and writing a question.
3. Pairs write their questions on index cards.
4. Teacher circulates and provides feedback.
5. When students complete the reading and writing of questions, the teacher collects the pair's index cards, reviews, and sorts them into the following categories: *Who, What, Where, Why* and *How* (see storyboard #7).
6. The next class period, the teacher draws a game board with *Who, What, Where, Why* & *How* as the categories.
7. The teacher places students in groups of four and provides each group with a whiteboard. Within each group, students are assigned a number from 1 to 4 (see storyboard #8).
8. Teacher poses a student-generated question and states, "Make sure every person on your team can give the correct answer."
9. In groups, students put their heads together, discuss, and answer the question.
10. Teacher randomly calls a number from 1 to 4. The student from each group whose number is called writes the group response on a whiteboard, then holds it up (see storyboard #9).
11. Teacher records points for each team with the correct response and asks questions until the game is complete.

Who, What, Where, Why & How

1

Today we are going to read the fable *The Elves and the Shoemaker*. To better understand what we read, we are going to use a question generation strategy called *Who, What, Where, Why & How*.

2

I've made a *Who, What, Where, Why & How* question poster. After I read each paragraph, I'll look at my poster and think of a question that starts with one of these words. Then, once I have my question, I'll write it down on an index card.

QUESTION POSTER

Who
What
Where
Why
How

3

Let me put the first paragraph of the story on the overhead and read it. Now, I'll look at my *Question Poster*. I'm going to write a *Why* question on my index card. Let's see, "Why did the shoemaker go to bed with a sad heart?"

The Elves & The Shoemaker

A shoemaker once lived in a little town. He was a good man and worked hard. But he became too poor to buy more leather. At last there was only enough for one pair of shoes. At night he cut out the shoes, but it was too late to make them. He put them on this bench and went to bed with a sad heart.

Question Poster

Who
What
Where
Why
How

Why did the shoemaker go to bed with a sad heart?

4

Let's read the second paragraph. OK, I need to look at my *Question Poster* again. This time, I'm going to write a *Who* question. "Who made the shoes?" Now, it's your turn. Use the *Question Poster* to think of another question. Share that question with a partner then write it on an index card.

The Elves & the Shoemaker (Paragraph 2)

In the morning, he went to finish them. But they were all done! Done inside and done outside! Now this surprised the good man. It made his eyes grow bigger and bigger. Who in the world could have finished the shoes?

Question Poster

Who
What
Where
Why
How

Who made the shoes?

Who, What, Where, Why & How

5

Let's generate one more question together before you work in pairs. First, read the paragraph. Second, look at the *Question Poster*. Last, write a question on your index card. After you write down your question, hold it up so I can check it.

The Elves & the Shoemaker (Paragraph 3)

Wife, he called, the shoes are done! Come and see. She ran to see. Sure enough, the shoes were all done and sitting on the shoemaker's bench. Then his wife's eyes grew bigger and bigger.

Question Poster

Who
What
Where
Why
How

Student Questions

Where did the people who made the shoes go?

Who made the shoes?

What made the shoemakers wife's eyes get bigger?

6

I can see that you can generate great questions using the *Question Poster*. Your job is to read the rest of the story with a partner. Remember to stop after every paragraph. Look at the *Question Poster* and write one question on each index card. I'm coming around to help.

QUESTION POSTER

Who
What
Where
Why
How

7

Excellent work using the *Who, What, Where, Why & How Poster* to write questions. I've collected all of your index cards and put them into columns on the whiteboard. The 100-point questions are easy, the 400-point questions are hard. We are going play a game where you work in teams to answer the questions you created.

Who	What	Where	Why	How
100	100	100	100	100
200	200	200	200	200
300	300	300	300	300
400	400	400	400	400

8

I've placed you in teams of four students. Your team should have a small whiteboard, dry erase marker, and eraser. Finally, each team member has been assigned a number from 1 to 4.

Who	What	Where	Why	How
100	100	100	100	100
200	200	200	200	200
300	300	300	300	300
400	400	400	400	400

TEACHER DESK

1	2
3	4

1	2
3	4

1	2
3	4

1	2
3	4

1	2
3	4

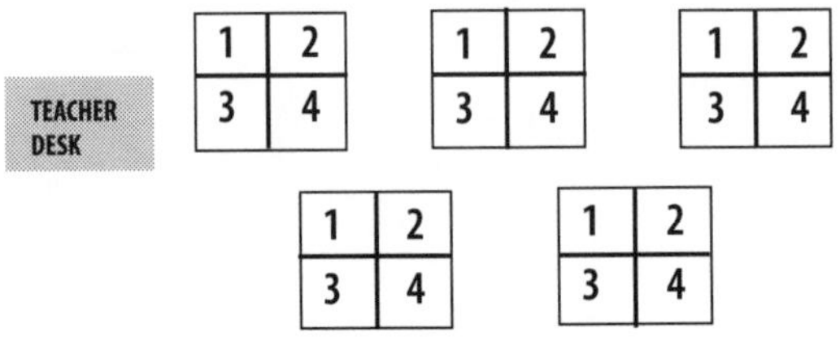

Who, What, Where, Why & How

9

I'm going to ask a question one of you wrote, and your group is going to put your heads together and come up with an answer. Then, I'm going to call a number. That number person is responsible for writing the answer on your group's small whiteboard. If you get the answer right, your group earns the points.

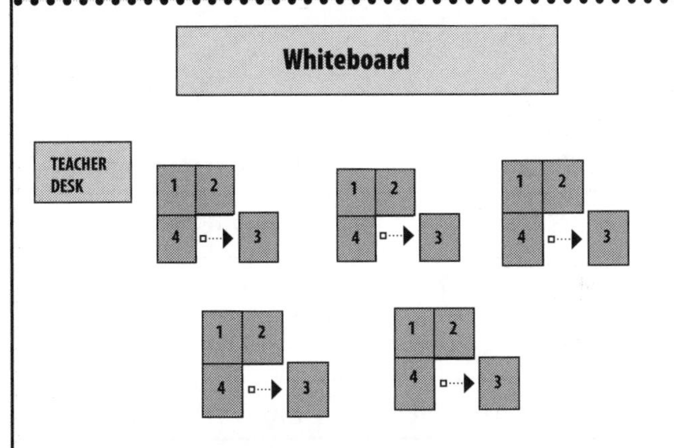

The first question is a **HOW** question for 100 points. "How did the shoes get made?" Put your heads together and discuss the answer. "Number 3's write the answer on your group's whiteboard. Number 3's show me your answer." The second question is a **WHY** question for 400-points. "Why didn't the elves make any shoes for themselves?"

STRATEGY 4:

Question Generation Matrix (Q-Trix)

This strategy is based on Chuck Wiederhold's Q-Structures research. Teachers consult a question matrix to label dice or make spinners that students use to help them generate a wide variety of questions before, during, and after they read.

Question Matrix

	Event	Character	Reasons	Resolutions
Present	What is?	Who is?	Why is?	How is?
Past	What did?	Who did?	Why did?	How did?
Predict	What will?	Who will?	Why will?	How will?
Imagine	What might?	Who might?	Why might?	How might?

If a teacher wants students to make predictions before they read, she may make a Prediction Spinner (see below) by incorporating the question stems from the predict row of the Question Matrix. In pairs, students will spin the spinner and generate a prediction question prior to reading each page. Similarly, if the class is studying characters in a story, reasons why certain things happen, or events, the teacher may create spinners by using the question stems in the columns under these categories. Then, after each page students spin the spinner and generate questions.

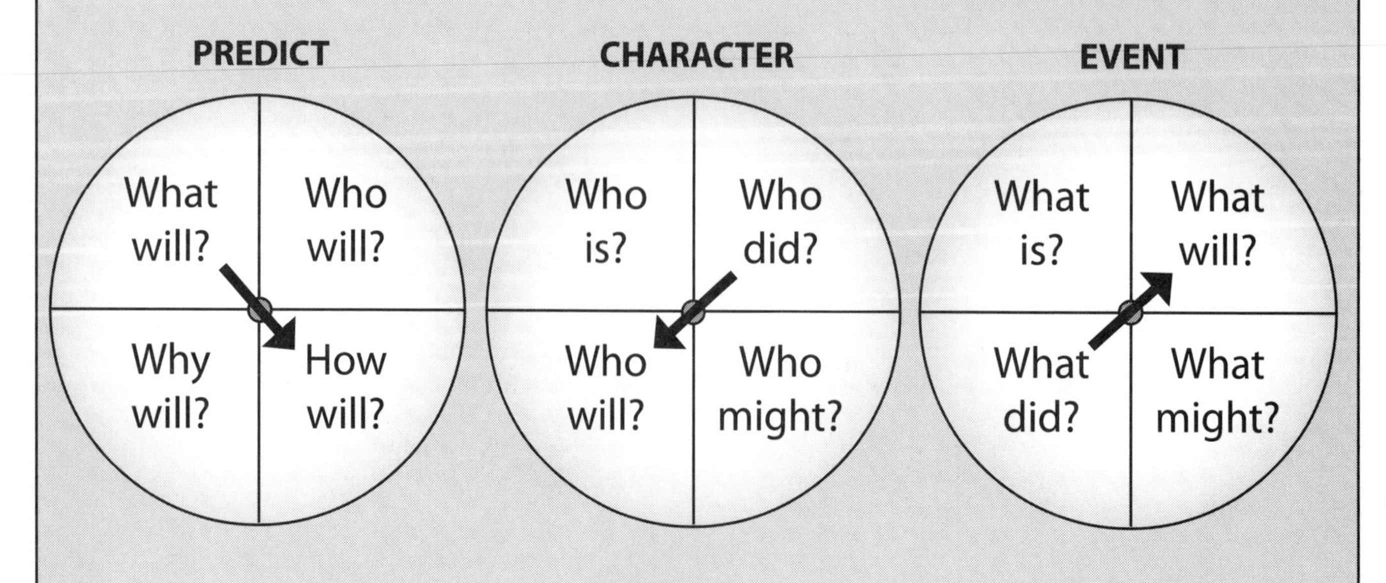

When teachers want students to generate questions about a variety of aspects of a story they may choose to put the Question Matrix on an overhead projector. During and after students read, the teacher may ask pairs to use the matrix to generate questions about the past, present and future. If the teacher is working with students on plot, she may ask dyads to develop a series of questions about reasons and resolutions. Or, if the teacher wants students to create questions about all aspects of a story, she may assign pairs to generate one question from each cell in the matrix.

A third way that teachers can get students to produce a variety of questions using the Question Matrix strategy is to label dice. On each side of one die, the teacher would glue one of the question words (Who, What, Why, How, Which and Where). On the other die, the teacher would glue the question verbs (is, did, can, would, will and might). After reading each page of a passage, the teacher may ask pairs to roll their dice and write a question based on the question stem produced by the top faces of the dice.

Step-by-Step

1. Prior to the lesson, the teacher determines how he is going to use the Question Matrix (i.e., spinner, whole matrix, dice), and what her focus is for students' question generation (event, character, reasons, resolutions, present, past, predict, or imagine).
2. The teacher places the Question Matrix on the overhead projector and informs students that as they read, they will use parts of this matrix to generate and answer questions they create.
3. The teacher states, "Today I want to focus our question generation on events that take place in chapter three of *Junie B. Jones Has a Peep in Her Pocket*.
   a. The teacher places the first page of the chapter students will read on the overhead projector along with an Event spinner.
   b. He reads the first two paragraphs.
   c. The teacher stops, spins the Event spinner and verbally generates a question. The teacher writes the question and then re-reads it to be sure that it makes sense.
   d. He reads the next two paragraphs.
   e. Again, the teacher stops, spins the Event spinner and verbally generates a second question. He writes the second question.
4. The teacher assigns students to pairs and distributes a copy of the story, an Event spinner, and index cards.
5. He instructs students that after every page, each person in the pair is to spin the spinner and use it to write down one question on an index card.
6. The teacher has pairs verbally answer each other's questions.
7. Students continue to generate and write questions on index cards for every page until they complete the chapter.
8. The teacher collects all index cards, shuffles them and then distributes them to pairs to answer.

References

Duffy-Hester, A.M. (1999). Teaching struggling readers in elementary school classrooms: A review of classroom reading programs and principles for instruction. *Reading Teacher, 52,* 480-495.

King, A. (1992). Comparison of self-questioning, summarizing, and notetaking review as strategies for learning from lectures. *American Educational Research Journal, 29,* 303-323.

King, A. (1994). Guiding knowledge construction in the classroom: Effects of teaching children how to question and how to explain. *American Educational Research Journal, 31,* 358-368.

Rosenshine, B., Meister, C., & Chapman, S. (1996). Teaching students to generate questions: A review of the intervention studies. *Review of Educational Research, 66,* 181-221.

Wiederhold, C. (1991). *Cooperative learning and critical thinking: The question matrix.* San Juan Capistrano, CA: Resources for Teachers.

Summarizing

2

1 Definition

If a picture tells 1,000 words, a summary condenses 1,000 words into 10. Students who write effective summaries identify main ideas, make associations between ideas, and relate the text to their own knowledge.

2 Chapter Preview

This chapter presents:

- Five summarizing strategies with accompanying visual lesson storyboards.
- Three videos of master teachers demonstrating these summarizing lessons.

3 Research

When students write summaries, they gain 30 to 100 percent more on recall and comprehension tests than students who re-read the text, underline, or answer questions at the end of a passage.

Notes

Composing Headings & Title Summaries

STRATEGY 1:

Composing Headings & Title Summaries

Having students write headings for each paragraph they read and a title for the entire passage, helps them identify the main ideas, then make associations between paragraphs and pages of the text.

Step-by-Step

1. Place a short piece of text on the overhead projector.
2. Make sure to white out the title and paragraph headings (see storyboard #1).
3. Read the first paragraph aloud and ask students to come up with possible headings. Write one of their suggested headings above the first paragraph (see storyboard #2). Read the next two paragraphs aloud, and repeat the process (see storyboards #3 and #4).
4. After modeling the strategy, assign a new text for students to read in pairs.
5. After every paragraph, ask students to write a two-to-three word heading (using Post-it Notes).
6. When headings for all paragraphs are complete, place students in groups of four and ask them to share and review their headings, then develop a title for the chapter (see storyboard #6).
7. Share titles with the whole class.

1

On the overhead is part of a story about the Madagascar aye-ayes. Our job is to come up with headings that capture the main idea for each paragraph and then think of a title that gives readers the big idea of the article.

Title:

Heading 1:

The aye-aye's odd-looking fingers, pointy teeth, big eyes, and huge ears give some people the creeps. Seeing an aye-aye is considered very bad luck to many residents of Madagascar, the African island country where these animals live in the wild.

Heading 2:

In parts of the country, people kill aye-ayes on sight, hoping to prevent anything "evil" from happening. The aye-aye's bad reputation isn't helped by the fact that it's active only at night, when things can seem a lot scarier to people.

Heading 3:

The truth about this five-pound animal, a type of lemur, is that it's harmless. Each one of its strange-looking characteristics helps an aye-aye survive. The little creatures are anything but scary. Aye-ayes are actually gentle, curious primates.

2

I'm going to read the first paragraph aloud, and while I'm reading, your job is to think of a heading, a two-to four-word title, that gives the main idea of the paragraph.

Heading 1: The Scary, Creepy Aye-Aye

The aye-aye's odd-looking fingers, pointy teeth, big eyes, and huge ears give some people the creeps. Seeing an aye-aye is considered very bad luck to many residents of Madagascar, the African island country where these animals live in the wild.

Composing Headings & Title Summaries

3

Excellent, heading! The first paragraph talked about the aye-aye's pointy teeth, big eyes and huge ears. It also discussed how people think they are bad luck. Let's read the second paragraph. Remember, while I read, you are thinking of a heading.

Heading 2: People Kill Night Aye-Ayes

In parts of the country, people kill aye-ayes on sight, hoping to prevent anything "evil" from happening. The aye-aye's bad reputation isn't helped by the fact that it's active only at night, when things can seem a lot scarier to people.

4

Yes, the main idea in the second paragraph is that people think aye-ayes are evil. So they kill them. Now read the third paragraph and come up with a heading on your own.

Heading 3:

The truth about this five-pound animal, a type of lemur, is that it's harmless. Each one of its strange-looking characteristics helps an aye-aye survive. The little creatures are anything but scary. Aye-ayes are actually gentle, curious primates.

5

Let's line up these three headings and think of a title for the whole article. We have *The Scary Looking Aye-Aye, People Kill Night Aye-Ayes*, and *Aye-Ayes Are Gentle*. Who has an idea? "The Scary Looking Gentle Aye-Aye!" Oh, I like that. That absolutely summarizes what we read. Do you see how this strategy works?

Title: The Scary Looking, Gentle Aye-Aye

Heading 1: The Scary, Creepy Aye-Aye

Heading 2: People Kill Night Aye-Ayes

Heading 3: Aye-Ayes Are Gentle

6

Now it's your turn. You are going to read an article about dolphins in pairs. First you'll write a heading for each paragraph. Once you finish writing the headings, you'll get into groups, compare your headings, and collaboratively create a title for the entire article.

Title:____________________________

Heading 1:____________________________

Rob Howes, his daughter Nicky, and two friends were swimming in the ocean. Suddenly a family of dolphins surrounded the swimmers. "The dolphins were going ballistic," said Howes. They were slapping the water with their tails. Then Howes saw big trouble--just six feet away was a great white shark.

Heading 2:____________________________

Too far from shore to outswim the predator if it attacked, Howes feared for the lives of the girls and himself. Gratefully, he realized that the dolphins' behavior was protecting them. The pod stayed with the swimmers for 40 minutes until it was clear that the danger had passed and the swimmers could make it to shore.

Place an Ad Summary

STRATEGY 2:

Place an Ad Summary

The goal of summarizing is to extract the most important information to capture the essence of a passage. What better way to do so than writing a classified ad, where more space costs more money.

Step-by-Step

1. Review the components of a newspaper, Web, or magazine classified advertisement. Present different examples to the class (see storyboards #2-4).
2. Pair students and have them read a passage/story.
3. Instruct students to imagine they are placing a classified ad to notify readers of the main ideas of the text.
4. Inform students that every word in their advertisement costs 10 cents, and they only have $3.50 to spend.
5. Challenge students to write the best possible summary advertisement using no more than 35 words (see storyboard #5).
6. Adjust the summary length by changing the amount of money students can spend.

1

Today, we are going to read the Grimm's fairy tale *The Little Red Cap*, and you are going to learn a fun strategy for how to summarize the big ideas in this story. The strategy is called *Place an Ad*.

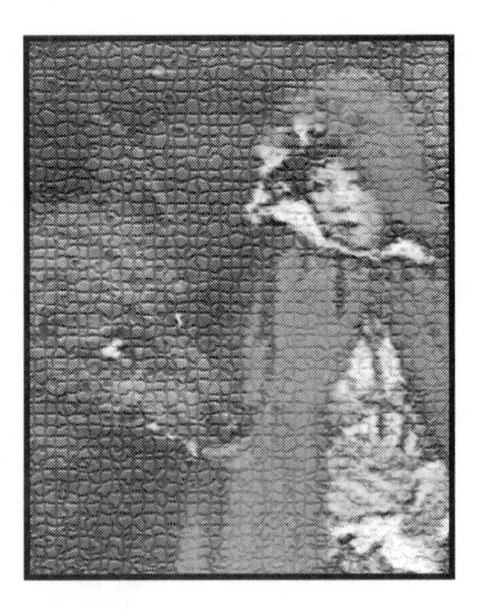

2

Has anybody ever read advertisements in the newspaper or on the Internet? What are some of the things people advertise? I'll make a list based on your answers.

Things People Advertise

Houses	Vacations
Cars	Drinks
Videogames	Food
Computers	Candy
Books	Jobs
Toys	Bikes
Restaurants	Skateboards

Place an Ad Summary

3

I've brought in some advertisements. The first is about an apartment for rent. In only 30 words, we see the number of bedrooms, baths and price. We also are informed that some items are new, there's lots of amenities, and who we should contact.

2BR/1BA APARTMENT $825
Remodeled with new floor, and extra storage area. Approx. 900 square feet. Amenities include: blinds, disposal, electrical stove, refrigerator, laundry room, heat and air.
Contact Dawn (209)555-1212

4

Here's another ad about an electronic toy. In 34 words we learn about the high resolution screen, 1 million puzzles, 5 levels, and small size.

Sudoku E-Puzzle

Comes with 1 million puzzles. Super high resolution LCD display. Five levels of play. Built-in clock with alarm. Measures four inches wide at the base and three inches at the top.

5

Today, you are going to write a 35-word advertisement for the fairy tale *The Little Red Cap*. But before you read this story, let me share a few advertisements I wrote to summarize two fairy tales we recently read.

CINDERELLA
PERSONALS: Girl in glass slipper looking for a prince. I'm gracious, modest, hard-working, and beautiful. If you marry me, we'll need extra room for my not-so-nice sisters.

SLEEPING BEAUTY
WANTED: A kind prince to awaken me from the wicked fairy's spell, then save me and our children from being eaten by your ogress mother.

6

Are you ready to write your own ad? These are your instructions: Remember, good advertisements condense lots of information to clearly communicate the key ideas of the product or services for sale.

PLACE AN AD

1. With a partner, read *The Little Red Cap.*
2. Write your advertisement.
3. Remember, every word costs 10 cents and you only can spend $3.50.
4. The ad that best communicates the fairy tale's big ideas and uses the least amount of money will earn an extra 10 minutes of recess.

Rule-Based Summaries

STRATEGY 3:

Rule-Based Summaries

The Rule-Based Summary strategy focuses students on implementing four rules: (1) eliminating redundant and irrelevant information, (2) paraphrasing, (3) extracting important ideas, and (4) relating text to their own knowledge.

Step-by-Step

1. Select and photocopy four different paragraphs for students to read and apply the Rule-Based Summary strategy.
2. For the first paragraph, the teacher uses an overhead projector to model each rule (see storyboards #2 and #3):
    - Delete unimportant information.
    - Replace a list with one idea.
    - Create a title.
    - Write a single-sentence summary.
3. For each subsequent paragraph, the teacher has students complete the final step, the final two steps, and then all steps (see storyboard #4).
4. The teacher then assigns a short text and students apply the Rule-Based Summary strategy to it independently (see storyboard #5).
5. Over time, the teacher assigns students longer and longer passages to apply the strategy.

1

Today, we are going to learn four rules for how to pull out the important ideas from paragraphs we read. Practicing these rules on several short paragraphs will help us use them when we read about desert adaptations in our science text later in the week.

2

These are the four rules for using the Rule-Based Summary strategy.

1. Delete unimportant information.
2. Replace a list of things with one idea.
3. Create a title.
4. Write a single-sentence summary.

I am going to read the paragraph on the overhead and show you how to apply each of these rules.

Title ____________________

The humpback whale is one of the rorquals, a family that also includes the Blue whale, fin whale, Bryde's whale, Sei whale, and Minke whale. Rorquals have two characteristics in common: dorsal fins on their backs, and ventral pleats running from the tip of the lower jaw back to the belly area. The shape and color pattern on the humpback whale's dorsal fin and flukes (tail) are as individual in each animal as are fingerprints in humans.

Summary Sentence ____________________

____

Rule-Based Summaries

3

The first thing I'll do is delete the unimportant parts. Next, I'll replace the words Blue whale, Fin whale, etc. with one word, WHALES. Then, I'll re-read the new paragraph and come up with a title. Finally, I'll write a sentence to summarize the entire paragraph.

1. Delete unimportant information.

2. Replace a list of things with a big idea.

3. Re-read the edited paragraph and create a title.

4. Write a single sentence to describe the paragraph.

***Title:* Humpback**

The humpback whale is one of the rorqual a family that also includes the Blue whale, Fin whale, Bryde's whale, Sei whale, and Minke whale (WHALES). Rorquals have two characteristics in common: dorsal fins on their backs, and ventral pleats running from the tip of the lower jaw back to the belly area. The shape and color pattern on the humpback whale's dorsal fin and flukes (tail) are as individual in each animal as are fingerprints in humans.

Summary Sentence

Rorqual whales (one of which is the humpback) have unique dorsal fins, flukes, and pleats.

4

Here is a different paragraph. Each of you has this paragraph in your packet. As you can see, I've completed rule 1 and rule 2 on the overhead. Your job is to complete rule 3 and rule 4.

3. Re-read the edited paragraph and create a title.

2. Replace a list of things with a big idea.

1. Delete unimportant information.

4. Write a single sentence to describe the paragraph.

Title ____________

NOBODY had ever seen anything like it. The two stray cats were always together. Not only that, one led the other wherever they went, with their tails entwined. How come? Unable to get close to them because they were so wild, a woman who looked after stray cats trapped the pair. That's when it was discovered that one cat was blind. A cloudy film covered his eyes. His sighted brother acted as his guide, hanging onto his tail and always stepping a bit ahead.

Summary Sentence

____

____

5

Let's try one more example before you practice on your own. I've made a chart to help you remember the rules.

RULE-BASED SUMMARIES

1. Delete unimportant information.
2. Replace a list with one idea.
3. Create a title.
4. Write a single sentence summary.

Title ____________

Albert Einstein, is not your ordinary pet goldfish. He has learned to take food from his owner's hand, swim through hoops, and even put a miniature soccer ball into a goal! It all started when Kyle Pomerleau, 9, won two goldfish at a school fair. Soon he noticed that the fish would react to his movements whenever he came near the tank. He and his dad decided to train Albert. They used techniques that work for other animals like dogs and killer whales.

Sentence Summary

____

____

4-2-1 Summary

STRATEGY 4:

4-2-1 Summary

This is an individual, cooperative, and whole class summarizing strategy.

Step-by-Step

1. Teacher assigns text for students to read.
2. After students read, the teacher asks them to individually write four things they learned from the passage (see storyboard #1).
3. Next, the teacher places students in pairs and instructs them to share their four ideas, then pick and record the two most important ideas (see storyboard #2).
4. Students are then placed in small groups where they study their ideas and collaboratively determine the one idea that best represents the most important learning (see storyboard #3).
5. To conclude the lesson, the teacher has each group report their idea out to the class. She records these ideas in a graphic organizer (see storyboards #4 and #5).

1

Today we are going to read a short biography of Michelle Kwan. While you read, you'll use a strategy called 4-2-1 Summary. On your desk is a 4-2-1 Summary Sheet. Your job is to individually write 4 reasons that made Michelle Kwan successful.

4-2-1 Summary Sheet

Write 4 reasons that made Michelle Kwan successful.

Write 2 reasons that made Michelle Kwan successful.

Write 1 reason that made Michelle Kwan successful.

2

Now that you have recorded 4 reasons individually, I'm going to place you in pairs. Discuss your ideas with a partner, and come up with 2 of the most important reasons why Michelle Kwan was successful.

Whiteboard

Teacher Desk

4-2-1 Summary Sheet

4 reasons why MK was successful | 2 reasons why MK was successful | 1 reason why MK was successful

4-2-1 Summary

3

As I walked around I heard some excellent ideas. It's time to form groups. In groups of four, collaboratively come up with the one big idea--the most important reason--that made Michelle Kwan successful.

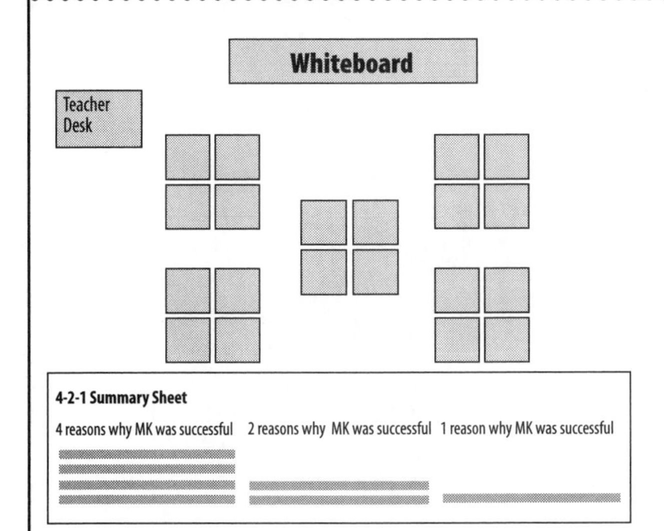

4

Group 1, what did you come up with? "She had great determination." Group 2? "She was self-motivated." You really have an eye for this. Let's hear from some other groups.

5

Group 3 what made Michelle Kwan successful? . . . . Now that we know the attributes that made Michelle Kwan successful, what makes you successful? List 4 reasons that make you successful.

Paragraph, Page, Passage Summary

STRATEGY 5:

Paragraph, Page, Passage Summary

This strategy requires students to generate headings for paragraphs, and then use those headings to construct page and passage summaries. It requires pupils to relate the ideas both within the text and between the text and their knowledge and experience.

Step-by-Step

1. The teacher places the first page of the text on the overhead projector.
2. He reads the first paragraph aloud, then stops, verbalizes his thinking, and writes a heading on a Post-it Note (see storyboard #2).
3. The teacher reads the second paragraph aloud and repeats the process (see storyboard #3).
4. When he gets to the bottom of the page, the teacher stops and re-reads his headings. Then, he writes a sentence or two that summarizes the information on the page (see storyboard #4).
5. The teacher assigns students reading partners and instructs them to write headings on Post-it Notes after every paragraph.
6. At the end of each page, the teacher reminds students to read their headings and write a page summary.
7. Finally, when students complete the passage, the teacher asks them to re-read their page summaries and write a passage summary.

1

We are going to begin our study of the Vikings by reading an overview article and using a comprehension strategy called *Paragraph, Page, Passage Summary* to help us remember key ideas. I'm going to model how to use this strategy, and then you'll work in pairs and use it while you read the article *Viking Voyages*.

2

On the overhead is the first paragraph of *Viking Voyages*. Let me read it to you, and after I read, I'll write a heading--on a small Post-it Note--that describes the big idea in the paragraph.

VIKING VOYAGES

For nearly 300 years, the Vikings sparked fear in their enemies. The Vikings were fearless warriors. They stormed villages, attacked fortresses, and stole gold. They even captured slaves. Not all Vikings, however, were villains. Some were farmers and craftspeople. Others discovered new lands. They were the first Europeans to sail to America. Yet their story is clouded in the mists of the past. Now it's time to meet the real Vikings.

Sailing Viking Thieves

Let's see. The paragraph was about how Vikings sailed, stole, fought, and attacked. It also said something about how some Vikings were farmers and craftspeople. Here's what I'll write on my Post-it Note.

3

Let's read the second paragraph.

VIKING VOYAGES

For nearly 300 years, the Vikings sparked fear in their enemies. The Vikings were fearless warriors. They stormed villages, attacked fortresses, andstole gold. They even captured slaves. Not all Vikings, however, were villains. Some were farmers and craftspeople. Others discovered new lands. They were the first Europeans to sail to America. Yet their story is clouded in the mists of the past. Now it's time to meet the real Vikings.

Sailing Viking Thieves

All stories have beginnings. This one is no different. It begins on June 8, 793. That's when Viking ships sailed toward a small island off the coast of England. It wasn't long before the island's inhabitants spotted the ships. It was impossible to see who was onboard. No one knew what was about to happen. No one knew that a new chapter in history was opening. They could only wait—and wonder.

793 Viking Invasion

Hmmm. In this paragraph there's not much information. I think I'll focus on when the first Viking ship landed in Europe. Let me write my second Post-it Note about that.

4

. . . Now that I have a heading for each paragraph, I need to read them to help me write a one-to two-sentence page summary. Notice how I write the page summary at the bottom on a larger Post-it Note.

VIKING VOYAGES

For nearly 300 years, the Vikings sparked fear in their enemies. The Vikings were fearless warriors. They stormed villages, attacked fortresses, and stole gold. They even captured slaves. Not all Vikings, however, were villains. Some were farmers and craftspeople. Others discovered new lands. They were the first Europeans to sail to America. Yet their story is clouded in the mists of the past. Now it's time to meet the real Vikings.

Sailing Viking Thieves

All stories have beginnings. This one is no different. It begins on June 8, 793. That's when Viking ships sailed toward a small island off the coast of England. It wasn't long before the island's inhabitants spotted the ships. They were still far away. It was impossible to see who was onboard. No one knew what was about to happen. No one knew that a new chapter in history was opening. They could only wait—and wonder.

793 Viking Invasion

The ships came closer. Each carried a hundred men. Some of the men used long oars. The oars plunged into the water. As the men pulled on the oars, the boats lurched forward. Alongside the oarsmen sat warriors. Each fighter wore a heavy metal helmet. Some carried swords. Others held axes. All were ready to take the island.

Fierce Warriors

In 793 Vikings invaded the English coast. Fierce warriors stole gold & captured slaves.

5

With a partner, you will read the rest of this article. After each paragraph you'll write a heading on a Post-it Note. When you get to the end of the page, read your headings and write a page summary. Finally, when you get to the end of the article, read all your page summaries and write a passage summary.

References

Bove, W., Bryman, A, Mars, R., Mayer, R.E., & Tapangco, L. (1996). When less is more: Meaningful learning from visual and verbal summaries of science textbook lessons. *Journal of Educational Psychology, 88*, 64-74.

Brown, A.L., Campione, J.C., & Day, J. (1981). Learning to learn: On training students to learn from texts. *Educational Researcher, 10,* 14-24.

Rosenshine, B. & Meister, C. (1995). *Scaffolds for teaching higher-order cognitive strategies*. In A.C. Ornstein (Ed., pp.134-153) Teaching: Theory into Practice. Boston: Allyn & Bacon.

Wittrock, M. (1990). Generative processes of comprehension. *Educational Psychologist, 24*, 345-376.

Wittrock, M. C. & Alesandrini, K. (1990). Generation of summaries and analogies and analytic and holistic abilities. *American Educational Research Journal, 27*, 489-502.

Text Structure

3

1 Definition

Most informational text is organized in one of seven ways (i.e., define, describe, compare, classify, order, cause/effect, or persuade). Conversely, narrative text is arranged around story sequence and story elements like setting, characters, plot, and theme. Teaching students to identify different text structures, and then how to organize and represent the information in the text, helps their comprehension immeasurably.

2 Chapter Preview

This chapter introduces

- nine strategies for how to teach students to recognize text structure, then organize and represent information within various texts.
- four videos of master teachers demonstrating how to teach: cause/effect, compare, persuade, and classify text structures.

3 Research

Students taught text structure strategies are able to extract major concepts, recall information, and apply what they learn. A review of the research showed that when students used text structure strategies to chunk, organize, and represent what they read, they performed 80 to 100 percent better on recall, comprehension, and problem solving tests.

Notes

Expository Text Structure

When writing expository prose authors determine where and when to define an idea, describe it, compare it to other similar or different ideas, or persuade readers to accept their point of view. These writing conventions are called **text structures**.

Interestingly, almost all informational text is organized around seven types of text structures. They are:

1) Define – a concept/idea is stated and followed by a definition.
2) Describe – a topic is introduced and followed by supporting details.
3) Order – a process is described sequentially.
4) Compare – two or more ideas are discussed and similarities and differences are highlighted.
5) Cause/Effect – a cause is stated followed by its concomitant effects.
6) Classify – objects, ideas, or items are categorized based on a set of common attributes.
7) Persuade – a position is put forth and supported by reasons and a conclusion.

Teaching students to identify different text structures is an important skill, because once they know an author's intention and organizing framework, it makes the ideas in the text easier to understand.

But recognizing text structure alone is insufficient for increasing one's comprehension. Teachers must also instruct students on how to extract and represent the most salient information they read. Doing so helps students see relationships between ideas and integrate new learning with their existing knowledge of the topic.

Step-by-Step

1. Explicitly communicate the organizing principle of the text students will read (e.g., definition, description, order, etc.).
2. Select the appropriate organizer and visually display the representation that students are going to use to extract and organize information.
3. Model how to use the graphic organizer. Read the beginning of the text whole class, and fill in part of the graphic organizer with student input.
4. After modeling, assign the selection (no more than a few pages) to groups of students or pairs, and ask them to fill out the graphic organizer.
5. Review group performance with the whole class to ensure groups extracted and organized the most salient information.
6. As students become more adept at identifying different text structures and using different types of graphic organizers, assign longer passages and more than one graphic organizer for them to use to organize the information they read.
7. After students complete their graphic organizers, develop a follow-up activity that gets them to study or use the information they organized.

Informational Text Structures

Definition Graphic Organizer

SEA TURTLES

The Loggerhead turtle is a large sea turtle with an exceptionally large head that measures 10 inches in diameter. It lives in warm waters near the tropics, the region of the world where the average annual temperature is higher and seasonal change is less dramatic than in other parts of the earth. Currently, Loggerheads are a threatened species; their population has dwindled over the past decade and they are now are in danger of extinction.

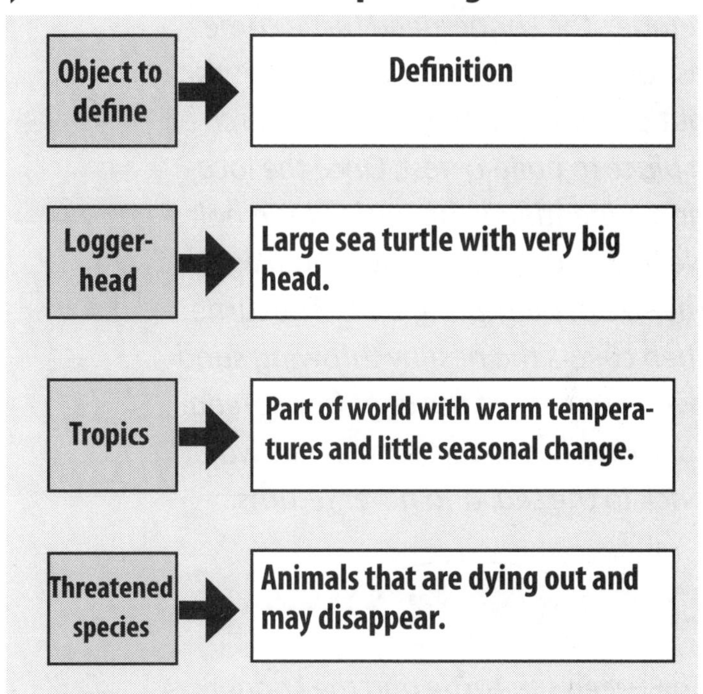

Description Graphic Organizer

With its reddish-brown upper shell and a dull yellowish lower shell, the adult Loggerhead weighs 200 to 350 pounds and lives in temperate waters. Loggerheads nest on the shores of the United States. They lay eggs in four to seven nests about 14 days apart. Over the course of one night female Loggerhead turtles can lay up to 130 eggs. The next morning they return to the sea and feast on shellfish, clams, horseshoe crabs, and jellyfish. The Loggerhead eggs hatch after incubating for 50 to 60 days.

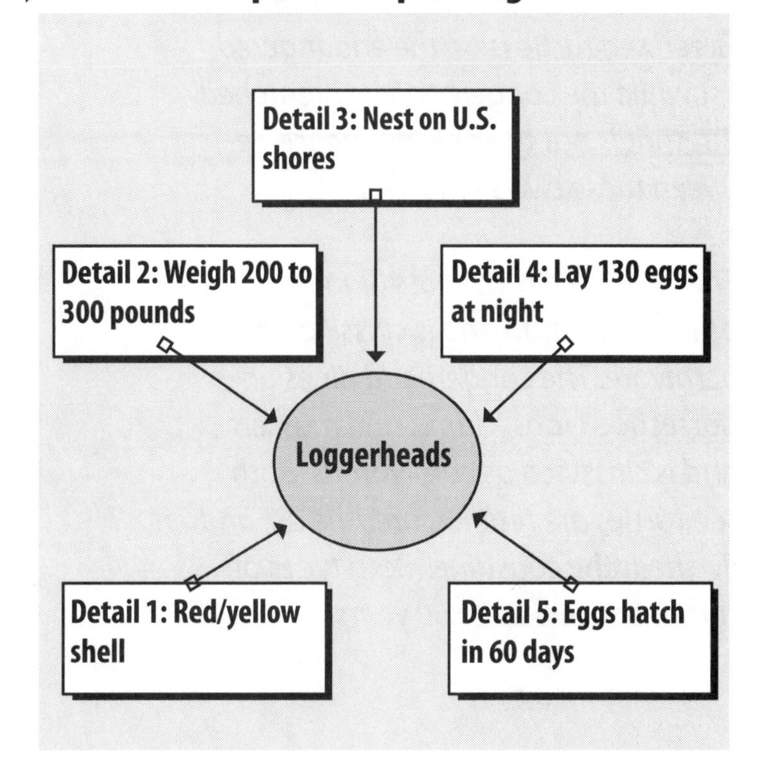

Informational Text Structures

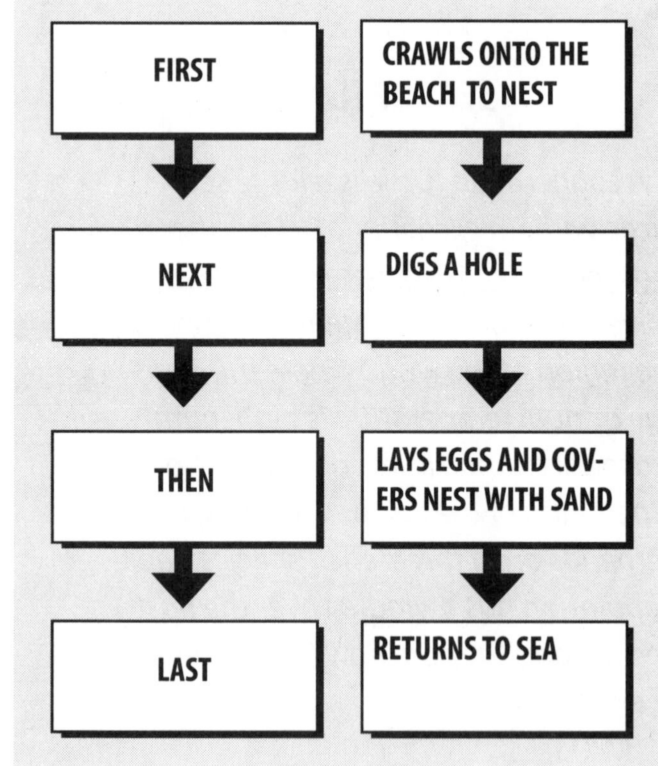

During the months from May to September, the Loggerhead turtle comes ashore to nest. First, the turtle crawls out of the sea to the beach in search of a place to build a nest. Once the location is identified, the turtle digs a hole. Next, the turtle lays around 120 eggs the size of ping-pong balls. The turtle then covers the nest by throwing sand over it to protect the eggs from predators. Finally, the turtle makes its way back to the sea, and never returns.

The Green sea turtle and the Loggerhead nest along the Atlantic and the Pacific shores in the United States. The Green sea turtle is on the endangered list while the Loggerhead is threatened. But that is not the only difference between these two sea turtles.

The Green sea turtle eats algae and other vegetation and is classified as a herbivore. The Loggerhead dines on horseshoe crabs, clams, and mussels and is classified as carnivorous. Both sea turtles are reptiles, breathe air, and live near the coastline. Both types of turtles can live up to 50 years.

Compare Graphic Organizer

Green Turtle
endangered
herbivore
eats algae

Similar
nest in U.S.
reptiles
breathe air
live 50 years

Loggerhead
threatened
carnivore
eats crabs

Informational Text Structures

Natural predators such as snakes, sea gulls, and raccoons are considered threats to sea turtles. But human beings pose the greatest threat of all. People disturb sea turtle nesting sites, which causes turtles to not lay eggs and return to the sea. Propellers and nets from fishing boats harm sea turtles, and human pollution in the ocean also puts them at risk. Finally, hunters sell turtle shells for jewelry and skin to make small leather items.

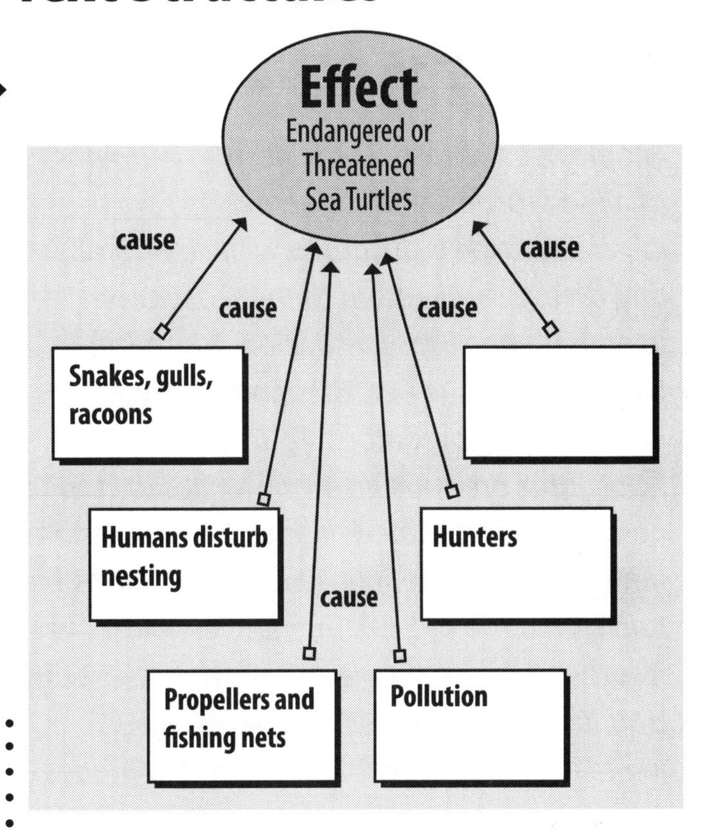

All sea turtles are cold-blooded reptiles. They breathe air and when active they must frequently resurface. Sea turtles have four flipper-like legs and a hard shell that is attached to their backbone. They cannot pull their head and legs into the shell.

Most sea turtles are carnivores (meat eaters), but the Green turtle is a herbivore (a plant eater that eats sea grass and algae). Carnivorous sea turtles feast on crustaceans (crabs, lobster, shrimp), shellfish, jellyfish, and small fish.

Adult female sea turtles return to the beach where they were born to lay their eggs. When the baby turtles hatch, they immediately head for the nearby water. Ninety-nine percent of baby turtles are eaten by birds and other predators during the trip from land to sea.

Categorize Graphic Organizer

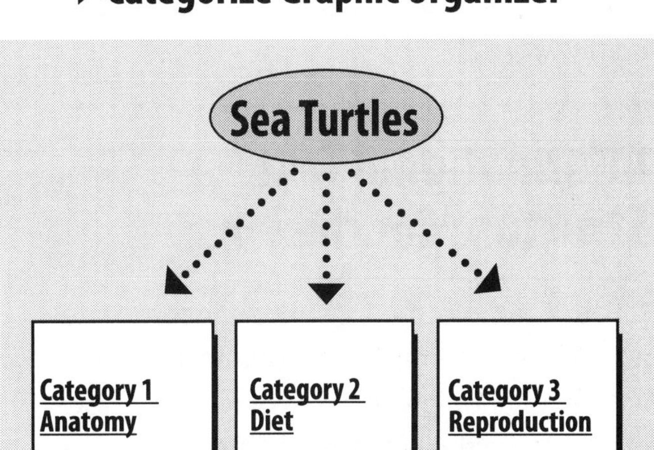

Informational Text Structures

People need to respect the nesting behaviors of all sea turtles, and Loggerhead in particular. If the turtle is disturbed while trying to find a nest, it will return to the sea without laying its eggs. This is especially alarming because only one percent of baby Loggerheads survive predators. Tourism and artificial lights are causing many turtles to stop nesting. Unfortunately, Lights Out policies are not enforced, so people have to be responsible and follow the policies themselves. Moreover, less than 50% of people visit nesting sites with trained and permitted individuals. By going to nesting sites without permitted guides people can unintentionally disturb nesting. If individuals continue to not respect the Loggerhead nesting sites, the reptiles may become extinct.

Persuasive Graphic Organizer

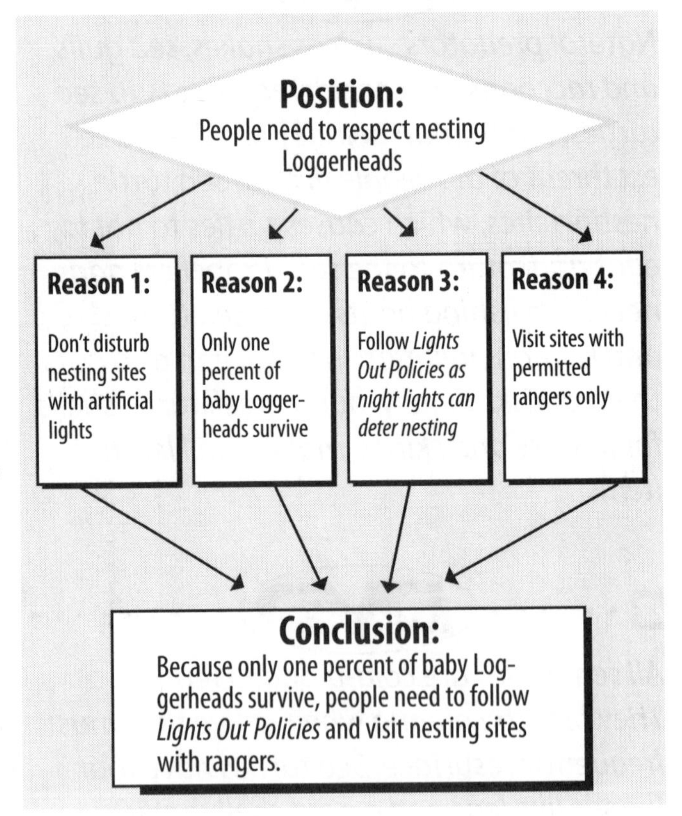

Informational Text Structure Conclusions

As our example shows, authors incorporate a variety of different types of text structures within any one given piece of writing. However, to effectively teach text structure strategies, teachers should focus students' attention on one text structure type (i.e., define, describe, order, compare, etc.) at a time so as not to overwhelm or confuse them.

Narrative Text Structure

Unlike informational text, students are more familiar with narrative prose because they learned to read using stories and fairy tales. Almost all narratives have characters, plot elements, settings, and themes. Moreover, most follow a story line with a beginning, middle, and end. To use text structure to increase students' comprehension of narrative prose, teachers will want to focus students' attention on:

(1) Story Elements: that is, the characters, setting, plot, and theme.
(2) Story Sequence: which consists of the beginning, middle, and end. In addition, some stories use flashbacks, or stream of consciousness where untangling the sequence takes considerable effort.

Step-by-Step

1. Decide to focus on either *Story Elements* or *Story Sequence* and select and display the graphic organizer that students are going to use (see examples).
2. For *Story Elements*, explicitly say that all stories have characters, settings, a plot and themes, and give examples of each of these ideas.
3. Model how to use the graphic organizer by reading a short text selection and soliciting whole-class student responses to fill it in.
4. After modeling, assign text to groups or pairs and ask them to fill in the graphic organizer.
5. Review group performance with the whole class to ensure students extracted and organized the most salient information.
6. After students complete their graphic organizers, assign an extended writing task that requires them to study and use the information they organized.

Story Elements

Text structure representations that organize story element information can include graphic organizers with all story elements (see first example), or a single element in greater detail (see examples for characters and plot). For shorter stories, teachers may want students to organize all elements in one representation. For longer narratives, teachers may require students to focus on a single element at a time.

Story Sequence

Story Sequence representations ask students to organize what happen in a narrative and in what order the events occurred (see example). These representations can address **time** (what happened in the beginning, middle, and end), **space** (where different parts of the story took place), and **character development** (how does a character change throughout the narrative).

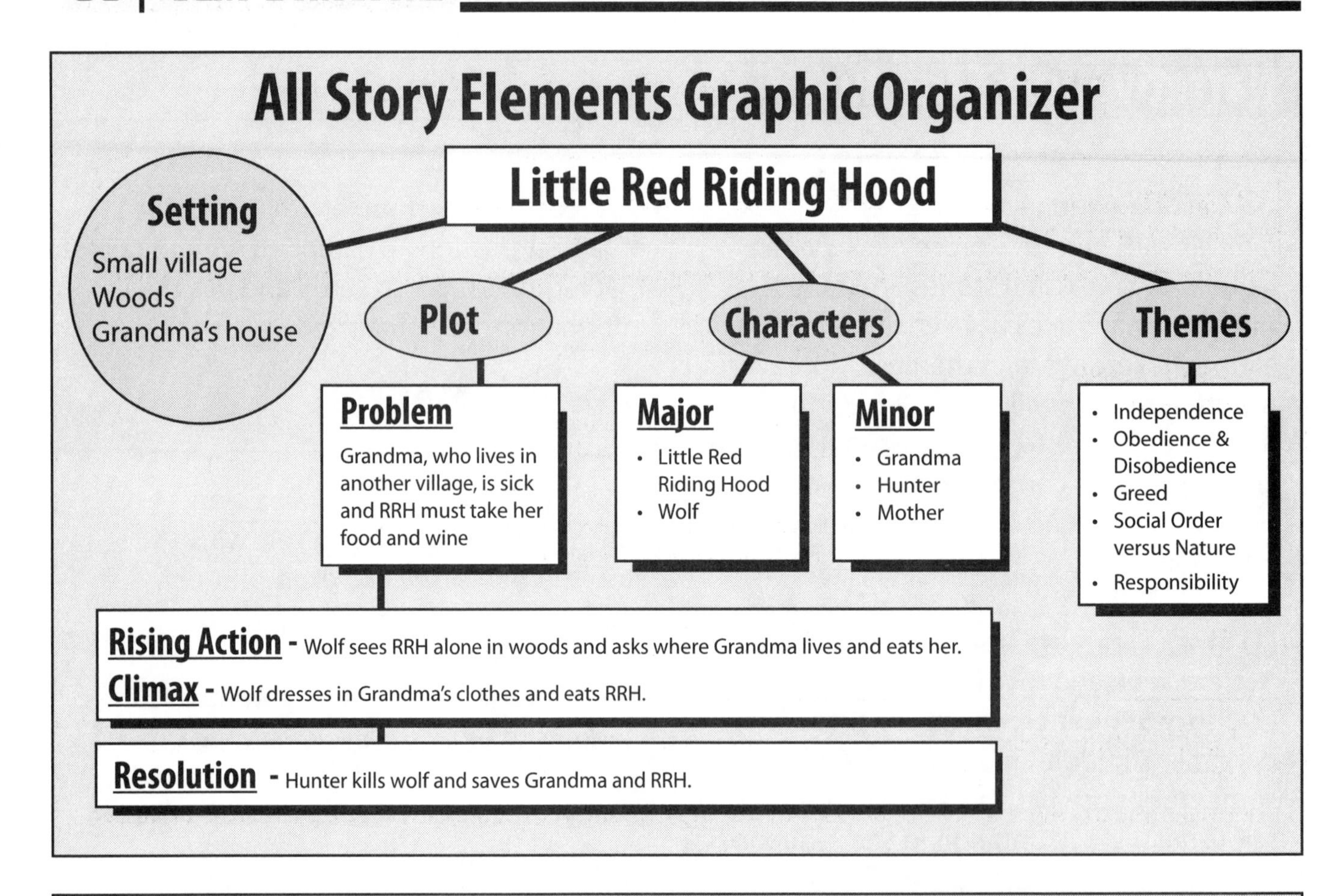

Character Story Element Graphic Organizer

Character	One Word Description	Appearance	Significance to the Story	Do you know anyone similar?
Grandma	Sick	White nightgown, night cap, reading glasses, lying in bed	RRH is bringing her food to help her feel better	I have a grandma, but she is not sick.
Wolf	Evil	Big ears, eyes, and sharp teeth	Tricks RRH and eats both her and her grandma	Sometimes strangers try to talk with you and trick you.
Red Riding Hood	Naive	Red cap, red shawl, apron, young girl	Takes her first trip alone to help her grandma and actually hurts her	Alyssa is really pretty and she sometimes wears a red baseball cap.
Mother	Caring	Blue apron and white blouse	Bakes cake and wine for RRH to take to help her grandma	My mom bakes the best cake and my dad sometimes makes wine, but I don't like it.
Hunter	Brave	Gun, knife, brown fur jacket, beard	Kills wolf and frees grandma and RRH	Police protect people from bad people and things.

Plot Story Element Graphic Organizer

Problem: Grandma is sick and Little Red Riding Hood must take her food and wine. Little Red Riding Hood has never walked to Grandma's house alone and her mother told her to stay on the path.

Events Leading to Resolution

- Little Red Riding Hood encounters a wolf. The wolf asks where she's going and RRH says to her grandma's house and tells the wolf how to get there.
- The wolf tells RRH about beautiful flowers off the path. While RRH is picking flowers, the wolf runs to Grandma's house and eats her.
- When RRH arrives at Grandma's the door is open and she senses something is wrong. The wolf, who is disguised as Grandma, tells RRH to come closer.
- The wolf eats RRH and falls asleep. His loud snoring causes a hunter who is passing by to go inside and check on Grandma.

Resolution: When the hunter sees that a wolf has eaten grandma, he takes a pair of scissors and cuts him open freeing Grandma and Little Red Riding Hood.

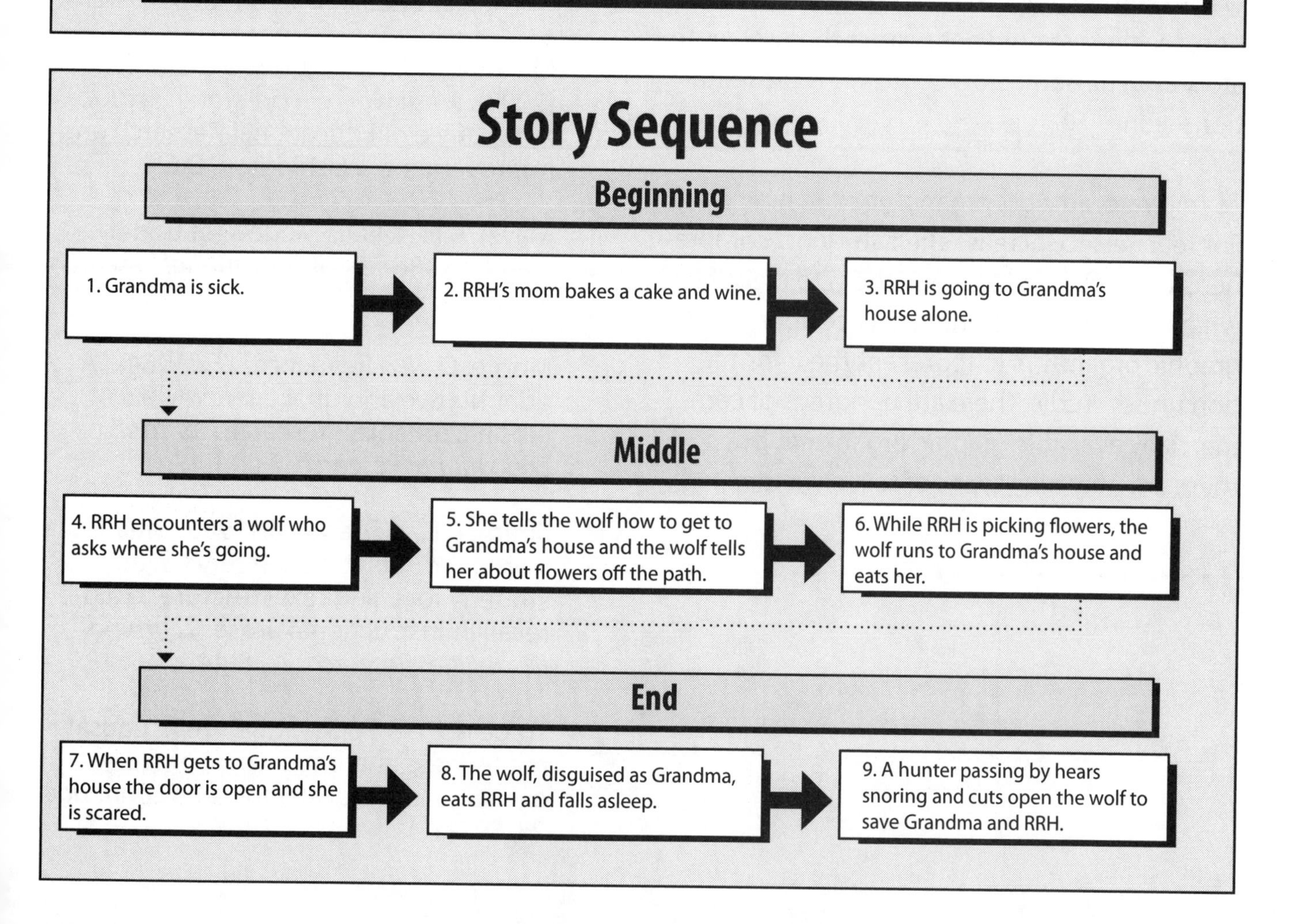

Chapter Review

In this chapter we introduced nine different types of text structures (seven for informational text and two for narrative text). However, many of the text structure representations for informational prose can be used to help students organize and comprehend narrative text as well.

In our videos, one master teacher uses expository prose to teach compare, cause/effect, and persuade text structures. In the other video, the teacher assigns the poem *The Highway Man* and requires her students to classify similes and metaphors.

This example shows that when reading fiction, teachers should not restrict themselves to *Story Structure* and *Story Sequence* representations alone.

To reiterate, authors organize text in nine ways. For teachers to increase their students comprehension, they need to teach them to identify what these ways are, and then use appropriate graphic organizers to represent the information under study. There are hundreds of commercially available graphic organizers, but there are only nine types of text structures.

References

Bacon, E. H., & Carpenter, D. (1989). Learning disabled and nondisabled college students' use of structure in recall of stories and text. *Learning Disability Quarterly, 12*, 108-118.

Bakken, J. P., Mastropieri, M.A., & Scruggs, T.E. (1997). Reading comprehension of expository science material and students with learning disabilities: A comparison of strategies. *Journal of Special Education, 31*, 300-324.

Cook, L. K. (1983). *Instructional effects of text structure-based reading strategies on the comprehension of scientific prose.* Unpublished doctoral dissertation, University of California, Santa Barbara.

Marzano, R.J., Gaddy, B.B. & Dean, C. (2000). *What works in classroom instruction.* Office of Educational Research and Improvement. Washington, D.C.

Mayer, R.E. (1989). Models for understanding. *Review of Educational Research, 59*, 43-64.

Moore, D.W. & Readence, J.E. (1984). A quantitative and qualitative review of graphic organizer research. *Journal of Educational Research, 78*, 11-17.

Smith, P. L., & Friend, M. (1986). Training learning disabled adolescents in a strategy for using text structure to aid recall of instructional prose. *Learning Disabilities Research, 2*, 38-44.

Trabasso, T. & Sperry, L.L. (1985). Causal relatedness and importance of story events. *Journal of Memory and Language, 24*, 595-611

Prior Knowledge

4

1 Definition

Good readers rely on what they know and experience to help them understand what they read. They use their prior knowledge before they read, and then compare and update that knowledge during and after reading.

2 Chapter Preview

This chapter presents

- four prior knowledge comprehension strategies with accompanying visual lesson storyboards.
- two videos of master teachers using the *Circle Map* and *CAA* prior knowledge strategies.

3 Research

The prior knowledge strategies described in this chapter increase recall, comprehension, and content learning between 17 and 32 percent. A recent review of more than 1,000 studies demonstrated that activating students' prior knowledge before and during instruction on average increased student achievement by 22 percent.

Notes

Circle Map

STRATEGY 1:

Circle Map

Circle Maps require students to list what they know about a topic and where they learned about it prior to reading. This exercise not only activates students' prior knowledge, but also helps them realize that knowledge comes from a variety of sources (e.g., school, a television show, the Internet, a family experience, a book, a friend, a teacher, etc.).

Step-by-Step

1. Write a question that gives students a hint about the topic they will read.
2. Distribute a *Circle Map* to every student, and have them write the topic word in the small center circle (see storyboard #1).
3. Instruct students to write everything they know about the topic in the large circle (see storyboard #2).
4. Ask students to think about where they learned the information they wrote in the large circle, and to record these ideas in the square section of the map (see example #3).
5. On the whiteboard, fill in a class *Circle Map* by soliciting student input (see storyboard #4).
6. Ask students to make predictions and then assign them to read the selection.

1

We are going to read a story about how to survive in the wilderness. Think for a moment about what you need to survive. Now, draw a *Circle Map* like mine, and write the word survival in the center.

2

Take three minutes and individually write down everything you need to survive in the big circle.

Circle Map

3

Think about where you learned all these things and record them in the square.

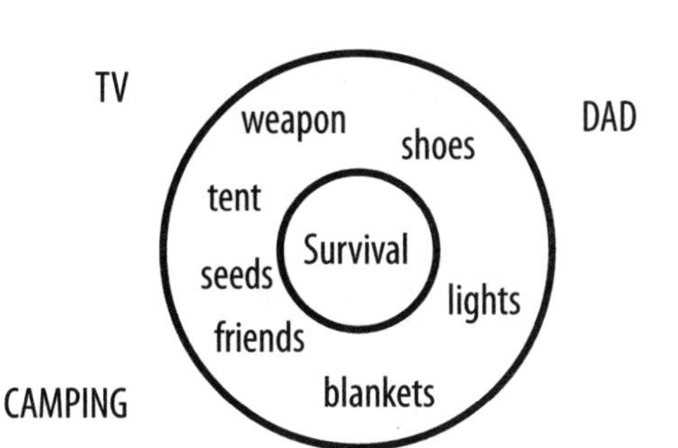

4

Now let's come back together and share some of these ideas on a big class *Circle Map*.

5

Great, we've recorded lots of ideas about survival. Use these ideas to write down three predictions of what you think might happen in the story we are about to read.

Predictions

1. People will get stuck in the wilderness.

2. A kid gets lost in the mountains.

3. Maybe it's about a family that lives out in the Bush in Alaska.

Anticipation Guides

STRATEGY 2:

Anticipation Guides

Anticipation Guides require students to answer and discuss controversial statements about a topic before they read a selection.

Step-by-Step

1. Teacher selects and pre-reads text.
2. He writes several thought provoking and/or controversial statements about the topic. Beside each statement, he provides a place for students to indicate whether they agree or disagree.
3. Students individually read each statement and check whether they agree or disagree (see storyboard #1).
4. Teacher assigns students to groups to discuss their responses (see storyboard #2) .
5. Students read in pairs and to revise their *Anticipation Guides* based on what they learned (see storyboards #3-4).

1

Before we start studying and reading about the legacy and cultures of American Indians, I want to see what you know. Take three minutes to individually complete the *Anticipation Guide* on your desk.

Agree	Disagree	Statement
		1. American Indians introduced horses to America.
		2. American Indians lost their land to European settlers because they did not unite as one tribe and fight together.
		3. Native Americans were hunters and gatherers.
		4. American Indians live in tepees.
		5. When American Indians got sick, they used herbal treatments, shamans, chants and dances to help cure disease.
		6. Native Americans have the same language, culture, beliefs and traditions.
		7. Today America Indians live on reservations.

In your table groups, discuss your answers for each statement. If you agree with the statement, give one reason why you think it's correct. If you disagree give one reason why you think it is incorrect.

Anticipation Guides

3

As I walked around, I heard some very interesting discussions about statements you agreed and disagreed with. It's time to read. With a partner, alternate reading each paragraph until you finish the chapter. As you read, fix your *Anticipation Guide* based on what you learn.

Agree	Disagree	Statement
✔		1. American Indians introduced horses to America.
✔		2. American Indians lost their land to European settlers because they did not unite as one tribe and fight together.
✔		3. Native Americans were hunters and gatherers.
	✔	4. American Indians live in tepees.
	✔	5. When American Indians got sick, they used herbal treatments, shamans, chants and dances to help cure disease.
	✔	6. Native Americans have the same language, culture, beliefs and traditions.
✔		7. Today America Indians live on reservations.

ANSWER CHANGE (statements 1, 3, 5, 7)

4

At your table, talk about the answers you changed based on what you learned from the text. We'll have a short class discussion when you finish. (STUDENT DISCUSSION STATEMENTS ARE IN ALL CAPS TEXT).

Agree	Disagree	Statement
	✔	1. THE SPANISH BROUGHT HORSES TO AMERICA.
✔		2. American Indians lost their land to European settlers because they did not unite as one tribe and fight together.
	✔	3. SEVERAL TRIBES GREW CROPS.
	✔	4. ONLY THE PLAINS INDIANS LIVED IN TEPEES.
✔		5. When American Indians got sick, they used herbal treatments, shamans, chants and dances to help cure disease.
	✔	6. Native Americans have the same language, culture, beliefs and traditions.
	✔	7. SOME INDIANS LIVE IN RESERVATIONS, SOME DON'T.

Concept Analysis Activity (CAA)

Strategy 3:

Concept Analysis Activity (CAA)

Generating examples and non-examples is a proven way to reinforce one's understanding of a concept. By asking students to generate examples and non-examples prior to reading and then re-categorize their examples after reading, teachers require students to use and update their knowledge.

Step-by-Step

1. Teacher pre-reads text and selects the concept she wants students to focus on.
2. Teacher writes the concept and underneath it she draws a T-Chart with the headings: Examples and Non-examples (see storyboard #3).
3. Teacher provides each student with dry erase boards, pens, and erasers.
4. Using their whiteboards students list as many examples of the concept that they can think of (see storyboard #3).
5. Students share their whiteboard ideas with the class, and the teacher writes several examples on her chart. Some examples will be incorrect; record them (see storyboard #3).
6. Next, students list non-examples on their whiteboards, and the teacher adds some of these to her class chart (see storyboard #4).
7. Students read the selection.
8. Teacher and students correct class chart, then students correct their charts (see storyboards #6-7).

1

Last week we studied reptiles. Can someone give me an example of a reptile that I can write on my CAA chart?

Reptiles	Non-Reptiles
Rattlesnake	
Iguana	
Boa constrictor	
Alligator	
Loggerhead turtle	
Crocodile	
Desert spiny lizard	
King snake	
Green turtle	
Leatherback turtle	

2

Great, now give me some non-examples to record.

Reptiles	Non-Reptiles
Rattlesnake	Ant
iguana	Pelican
Boa constrictor	Tree frog
Alligator	People
Loggerhead turtle	Lobster
Crocodile	Monkey
Desert spiny lizard	Elephant
King snake	Rat
Green turtle	Fish
Leatherback turtle	Shark

CAA: Mammals

3

This week, we're going to read and learn about mammals. Take out your whiteboards, and draw a T-Chart. On the left write mammals. On the right side write non-mammals. Take three minutes and write down as many examples of mammals as you can. It is ok if you are not sure. Feel free to guess. Now lets record some of your ideas.

Mammals	Non-mammals
Whales	
Human	
Apes	
Ducks	
Dogs	
Seals	
Birds	
Tigers	
Elephants	
Frogs	
Lion	

4

CAA: Mammals

As I was walking around, I saw some great examples. Take two minutes and under non-mammals, write animals that you think are NOT mammals. Ok, let's record some of your ideas on the class chart.

Mammals	Non-mammals
Whales	Ants
Human	Bats
Apes	Frogs
Ducks	Lizard
Dogs	Snakes
Seals	Rats
Birds	Sharks
Tigers	Alligator
Elephants	Sharks
Frogs	Turtles
Lion	Kangaroos

5

Read Lesson

Let's read about mammals to see if our examples and non-examples are correct. Take 20 minutes to read the chapter with a partner. As you read, be thinking about what things or qualities make a mammal a mammal. Talk about these qualities with your reading buddy.

Concept Analysis Activity (CAA)

6

Now that we've read about mammals, can someone tell me what things make a mammal a mammal? I'll write them in a corner box next to our class CAA Mammal Chart. Now let's use these qualities to see if our examples and non examples of mammals are correct.

Mammals	Non-mammals
Whales	Ants
Human	Bats
Apes	Frogs
Ducks	Lizard
Dogs	Snakes
Seals	Rats
Birds	Sharks
Tigers	Alligator
Elephants	Sharks
Frogs	Turtles
Lion	Kangaroos

ATTRIBUTES OF MAMMALS

HAIR
NURSE YOUNG
LIVE BABIES
WARM BLOODED

Do ducks or birds nurse their young?

Do bats and rats have live babies and nurse their young?

Kangaroos have live babies, nurse their young, and have hair.

Do frogs have hair?

CAA: MAMMALS

7

So here is our final CAA Mammals Chart. Now that you know the qualities of what makes a mammal a mammal fix your chart before the end of the lesson.

Mammals	Non-mammals
Whales	Ants
Human	Ducks
Apes	Frogs
Bats	Lizard
Dogs	Snakes
Seals	Birds
Rats	Sharks
Tigers	Alligator
Elephants	Sharks
Kangaroos	Turtles
Lion	Frogs

STRATEGY 4:

Semantic Feature Analysis (SFA)

The Semantic Feature Analysis strategy activates students' prior knowledge by requiring them to make hypotheses about relationships between ideas in the text, and then read to confirm, modify or disconfirmed their guesses.

Step-by-Step

1. Teacher pre-reads text and lists the major ideas in the top columns of the SFA Matrix (see storyboard #1).
2. Next, the teacher identifies examples of the major ideas and lists those down the first column of the matrix.
3. Teacher inserts a legend (**+** = positive relationship, **-** = negative relationship, **?** = uncertain).
4. Teacher photocopies and distributes a SFA matrix to every student.
5. Students read the examples in the matrix and make hypotheses about the relationships between each example and each big idea before reading (see storyboard #2).
6. After students complete the matrix, they read the passage to confirm hypotheses, clarify relationships that were unknown, and modify relationships that were disconfirmed by the text (see storyboards #3-4).

Semantic Feature Analysis (SFA)

1

Today we are going to learn about the different rules that govern the U.S. Senate and House. Before we begin, I want to see what you know about the House and Senate, so I created this matrix. Notice that there are columns for the House and Senate. There are also 10 statements. I want you to read each statement and predict if it applies to the House, Senate, or both branches. Let's do the first one together.

+ = positive relationship
- = negative relationship
? = not sure

	House of Representatives	Senate
1. Members elected every two years	+	–
2. Thirty-five year age limit		
3. Members elected every six years		
4. Representatives determined based on state's population		
5. Representative must be inhabitants of state		
6. Twenty-five year age limit		
7. Power to remove president from office		
8. Two representatives per state		
9. Has the sole power of impeachment		
10. Vice president presides		

2

Do you see how this works. Now, I'd like you to individually read each statement and predict whether it relates to the House, Senate, or both. If you're not sure, use a "?". After you make all your predictions, you'll read *Article 1* of the *U.S. Constitution* and make corrections where your predictions were off.

+ = positive relationship
- = negative relationship
? = not sure

	House of Representatives	Senate
1. Members elected every two years	+	–
2. Thirty-five year age limit	–	+
3. Members elected every six years	–	+
4. Representatives determined based on state's population	–	+
5. Representative must be inhabitants of state	+	+
6. Twenty-five year age limit	+	–
7. Power to remove president from office	?	?
8. Two representatives per state	+	–
9. Has the sole power of impeachment	?	?
10. Vice president presides	?	?

Semantic Feature Analysis (SFA)

3

When you make your corrections after you read, make sure you highlight what your corrections are and jot down what you learned.

+ = positive relationship
- = negative relationship
? = not sure

	House of Representatives	Senate
1. Members elected every two years	+	−
2. Thirty-five year age limit	−	+
3. Members elected every six years	−	+
4. Representatives determined based on state's population	+	−
5. Representative must be inhabitants of state	+	+
6. Twenty-five year age limit	+	−
7. Power to remove president from office	?	?
8. Two representatives per state	−	+
9. Has the sole power of impeachment	+	−
10. Vice president presides	−	+

Student identifies errors after reading

#4 and #8 – Senate has only two members per state and House members based on state's population.
#7 – House impeaches, but it take 2/3rds of the Senate to to remove the President.
#10 – I learned the VP sits in the Senate and can cast the deciding vote if it's 50/50.

4

Now that you've updated your SFA Matrix after reading Article 1, let's see if you are correct. Get into groups of four. When I say pass your paper, each person pass their paper to the right. The person who receives that paper determines if the relationship for number 1 was correct. If yes, they put a check, if no, they circle it. After you pass the paper 10 times, return it to the original owner.

References

Anders, P. L. & Bos, C. S. (1986). Semantic feature analysis: An interactive strategy for vocabulary development and text comprehension. *Journal of Reading, 29*, 610-616.

Bos, C., Anders, P., Filip, D. & Jaffy, L. (1989). The effects of an interactive instructional strategy for enhancing reading comprehension and content area learning for students with learning disabilities. *Journal of Learning Disabilities, 22*, 384-390.

Bransford, J. D. & Johnson, M. K. (1972). Context prerequisites for understanding: Some investigations of comprehension and recall. *Journal of Verbal Learning and Verbal Behavior, 11*, 717-726.

Duffelmeyer, F. (1994). Effective anticipation guide statements for learning from expository prose. *Journal of Reading, 37*, 452-455.

Marzano, R.J., Gaddy, B.B. & Dean, C. (2000). *What works in classroom instruction.* Office of Educational Research and Improvement. Washington, D.C.

Sachs, A. (1983). The effects of three prereading activities on learning disabled students' reading comprehension. *Learning Disability Quarterly, 6*, 248-251.

Comprehension Monitoring

5

1 Definition

Effective readers are aware of how difficult or easy a text is, how much they know about the ideas, and to what degree they are understanding. Before reading, they set goals and preview. During reading, they ask questions, adjust their reading speed, and re-read difficult parts. After reading, they summarize, answer questions, and clarify ideas.

2 Chapter Preview

In this chapter we present

- four comprehension monitoring strategies with accompanying visual storyboards.
- two videos of master teachers demonstrating the *Fix-Up* and *IEPC* strategies.

3 Research

In a review of 11 studies that related comprehension monitoring to reading outcomes, all investigations showed positive relationships between high-monitoring readers and increased comprehension test scores. A recent review of the research reported that teachers who taught their students how to monitor their comprehension produced students who performed 25 percent better on standardized tests.

Notes

Fix-Up Strategies

STRATEGY 1:

Fix-Up Strategies

When a capable reader's comprehension is failing, instead of continuing to read, he or she uses a variety of *Fix-Up Strategies* to improve his or her understanding.

Step-by-Step

1. Review the *Fix-Up Strategy* poster and give each student *a Fix-Up Strategy Checklist* (see storyboard #1).
2. Prior to reading, model the *Before Reading Fix-Up Strategies* (see storyboard #2).
3. Then, using an overhead projector, read the first two paragraphs from the passage aloud and model how to use two of the *During Reading Fix-Up Strategies* (see storyboard #3).
   a. Stop after reading two paragraphs.
   b. Refer to *Fix-Up Strategies* and think aloud: "I'm going to write a heading. Writing headings, helps me monitor my comprehension."
   c. Read two more paragraphs, refer to *Fix-Up Strategies* and think aloud: "Hmmm, I don't know what these two words mean so I'll underline them and look them up to clarify my understanding."
   d. Teacher repeats steps ***a*** to ***c***, modeling more examples of these two strategies.
4. Teacher assigns text for students to read and reminds them to check off the *Fix-Up Strategies* they use while reading.
5. When students complete the reading, they share reflections about the *strategies* they used and how they were helpful.

1

Good readers monitor their comprehension while they read. To do this, they use strategies before, during and after reading. On the overhead is a Fix-Up Strategy Checklist. Today, we are going to learn how to use some of these strategies while we read.

Fix-Up Strategy Checklist

	1. Before Reading
____	**Preview** - skim title, pictures, tables, diagrams & questions
____	**Predict** what might happen
____	**Purpose** - What is my purpose for reading this?
	2. During Reading
____	**Ask Questions** - use who, what, where, when,why & how stems
____	**Write Headings** - three to five word titles for each paragraph
____	**Visualize** by drawing a picture of what you read
____	**Underline** unfamiliar words, then look them up
	3. After Reading
____	**Summarize** - in two to three sentences write the main idea
____	**Re-read** the parts you did not understand
____	**Answer** the questions you asked

Fix-Up Strategies

2

Since we've been studying about health, I'm going to show you how to use *Fix-Up Strategies* while I read this article aloud. Then, you'll read an article and use the strategies I modeled. The first thing I'll do is **Preview** this article. I don't see any pictures, diagrams or charts, but I do see a title. I'll use the title to make a **Prediction**.

Super Foods ☐ ······▶ **I predict this article will be about foods that give you energy.**

SOME VEGGIES FIGHT CANCER

Research now shows some foods, including tomatoes, onions, garlic, and olive oil are among the superfoods. Superfoods are packed with powerful chemicals that may offer your body great protection against disease -- including cancer, obesity, and heart disease.

Natalie Ledesma, a registered dietician, says compounds found in super foods can boost the immune system and even protect the heart. Here is what she shops for.

EAT HERBS & SPICES

Herbs! "Dark green ones, like rosemary and thyme, and any intensely colored spice, like turmeric or red pepper. Both of those have anti-inflammatory properties."

Fix-Up Strategy Checklist

	1. Before Reading
X	Preview - skim title, pictures, tables, diagrams & questions
X	Predict what might happen
____	Purpose - What is my purpose for reading this?
	2. During Reading
____	Ask Questions - use who, what, where, when, why & how stems
X	Write Headings - three to five word titles for each paragraph
____	Visualize by drawing a picture of what you read
____	Underline unfamiliar words, then look them up
	3. After Reading
____	Summarize - in two to three sentences write the main idea
____	Re-read the parts you did not understand
____	Answer the questions you asked

Notice how after I read each paragraph, I stop, think, and write a **Heading**. This strategy helps me remember the big ideas in that paragraph. Watch how I check off the three *Fix-Up Strategies* I used.

3

Now I'll read the next page and again use my *Fix-Up Strategies Checklist*. I'm going to continue to **Write Headings** for paragraphs as this strategy helps me understand and remember what each paragraph is about.

Super Foods (page 2)

RED PEPPERS REDUCE CANCER

Turmeric may reduce the risk of **leukemia**, skin, and liver cancers. Hot peppers may reduce the risk of colon, stomach, and **rectal** cancers. Also on the list: green veggies, but not just any green veggies.

BRUSSEL SPROUTS FIGHT CANCER

"Brussel sprouts are part of the **cruciferous** vegetable family that has significant anti-cancer properties," said Ledesma. Other cruciferous veggies include cabbage, broccoli, and cauliflower. And don't forget the tomato's anticancer properties, especially with **prostate** and potentially lung and breast cancer.

BERRIES PREVENT VIRUSES

As for fruit, citrus contains Vitamin C, and **phenols**, which inactivate cancer cells and strengthen the immune system. Cantaloupes, mangos, and carrots contain cancer-fighting **carotenoids.** And berries are bursting with **flavonoids** and **ellagic acid** -- **antioxidants** that protect against cancer, ulcers, and viruses.

Fix-Up Strategy Checklist

	1. Before Reading
X	Preview - skim title, pictures, tables, diagrams & questions
X	Predict what might happen
____	Purpose - What is my purpose for reading this?
	2. During Reading
____	Ask Questions - use who, what, where, when, why & how stems
X	Write Headings - three to five word titles for each paragraph
____	Visualize by drawing a picture of what you read
X	Underline unfamiliar words, then look them up
	3. After Reading
____	Summarize - in two to three sentences write the main idea
____	Re-read the parts you did not understand
____	Answer the questions you asked

When I read this page, I noticed that there were a lot of words that I didn't understand. So, I decided to underline them and I'll look them up when I finish reading the page.

Fix-Up Strategies

4

Do you see how I'm using the *Fix-Up Strategies Checklist* to help me monitor my comprehension? Let's have you practice. First, with a partner, **Preview & Predict**. Then, as you read, use the **Write Headings** and **Underline** strategies. If you use other strategies, make sure to check them off on your list. I'm coming around to provide feedback and skim your checklists to see which *Fix Up Strategies* you are using.

Mercury in Fish

For someone who watches her diet as much as Wendy Moro, the symptoms didn't add up. "I had severe fatigue and vertigo. I was at one point able to leg press two hundred pounds, (but) I could barely walk down the block," she says.

Why, she wondered, would someone who eats so healthily feel so unhealthy? Wendy claimed doctor after doctor misdiagnosed her condition. Then, Wendy and her current doctor begin to suspect the answer was on her plate.

"A few times a week I was having fish, whether it was once or three times or four times," says Wendy.

"What kind of fish? Swordfish, ahi, tuna and sea bass, the highest mercury-content fish sold in the commercial market," says Dr. Jane Hightower. Wendy's symptoms were caused by what she was eating.

Fix-Up Strategy Checklist

1. Before Reading

_____ Preview - skim title, pictures, tables, diagrams & questions

_____ Predict what might happen

_____ Purpose - What is my purpose for reading this?

2. During Reading

_____ Ask Questions - use who, what, where, when,why & how stems

_____ Write Headings - three to five word titles for each paragraph

_____ Visualize by drawing a picture of what you read

_____ Underline unfamiliar words, then look them up

3. After Reading

_____ Summarize - in two to three sentences write the main idea

_____ Re-read the parts you did not understand

_____ Answer the questions you asked

Image, Elaborate, Predict & Confirm

STRATEGY 2:

Image, Elaborate, Predict & Confirm (IEPC)

Using the IEPC strategy, students imagine, elaborate, and make predictions before reading. Then, they read to confirm or disconfirm their elaborations and predictions.

Step-by-Step

1. Display the IEPC chart on an overhead projector and describe what each letter in IEPC stands for (Image, Elaborate, Predict, Confirm).
2. Using a short text selection or book students are highly familiar with, model each of the IEPC processes by filling out a chart with whole class input (see storyboards #1-5).
3. Assign a new text and arrange students in groups of four. Designate a leader for each group. The leader is responsible for recording the group's Images, Elaborations, and Predictions in the IEPC chart prior to reading (see DVD teaching example).
4. As students read, the leader stops and with group input writes down interesting ideas and facts.
5. After reading the group discusses which predictions were correct and fixes those that were not (see DVD teaching example).

1

Today, we are going to combine several reading comprehension strategies into one strategy called IEPC. IEPC stands for Image, Elaborate, Predict & Confirm. This strategy is going to help us monitor our understanding of the story, *Wolf.* Close your eyes. When you hear the title, *Wolf,* what do you see, hear, smell and feel. Let's record some of those images.

IEPC CHART

I = IMAGE	E = ELABORATE	P = PREDICT	C = CONFIRM
• Scary • big hairy • chases people • big teeth • hides in bushes • black eyes • drooling • Other animals are afraid • Night • Howling • Full moon • Chases animals			

2

Now turn to a partner, discuss your images, and add some details to bring them to life. I'll do the first one. Ok, let's share some elaborations with the class. I'll record them on our class IEPC chart.

IEPC CHART

I = IMAGE	E = ELABORATE	P = PREDICT	C = CONFIRM
• Scary • big hairy • chases people • big teeth • hides in bushes • black eyes • drooling • Other animals are afraid • Night • Howling • Full moon • Chases animals	• I see a big black ferocious wolf showing its teeth • He is growling and licking his lips, as he corners a child • He is hungry and pacing back and forth • He is about to pounce on someone • He wants to eat the pigs. • Hunters will probably kill him • He is running in the snow with a pack of friends in the moonlight.		

Image, Elaborate, Predict & Confirm

3

Those are some great elaborations. Let's do one more thing before we read. Look at this picture on the title page of the book, and write down two predictions about what you think is going to happen in this story.

IEPC CHART

I = IMAGE	E = ELABORATE	**P = PREDICT**	C = CONFIRM
• Scary • big hairy • chases people • big teeth • hides in bushes • black eyes • drooling • Other animals are afraid • Night • Howling • Full moon • Chases animals	• I see a big black ferocious wolf showing its teeth • He is growling and licking his lips, as he corners a child • He is hungry and pacing back and forth • He is about to pounce on someone • He wants to eat the pigs. • Hunters will probably kill him • He is running in the snow with a pack of friends in the moonlight.	• He is not a real wolf, just a story book wolf, I don't think he is going to eat anyone. • He looks like Gunnywolf, maybe he'll sing songs. • I think he is going to read to the animals instead of eating them. • After he reads, everyone will be happy. • He is not going to be mean. • Maybe he will trick the animals.	

4

There are a lot of interesting predictions. Let's read. While we read, we'll be looking for interesting ideas to write down. Record these ideas in the Confirm column.

IEPC CHART

I = IMAGE	E = ELABORATE	P = PREDICT	**C = CONFIRM**
• Scary • big hairy • chases people • big teeth • hides in bushes • black eyes • drooling • Other animals are afraid • Night • Howling • Full moon • Chases animals	• I see a big black ferocious wolf showing its teeth • He is growling and licking his lips, as he corners a child • He is hungry and pacing back and forth • He is about to pounce on someone • He wants to eat the pigs. • Hunters will probably kill him • He is running in the snow with a pack of friends in the moonlight.	• He is not a real wolf, just a story book wolf, I don't think he is going to eat anyone. • He looks like Gunnywolf, maybe he'll sing songs. • I think he is going to read to the animals instead of eating them. • After he reads, everyone will be happy. • He is not going to be mean. • Maybe he will trick the animals.	• He looks like a wolf, but he goes to school. • He starts off being mean. • He tries to scare the animals by howling and jumping. • Everyone is happy at the end. • Only the chickens and rabbits run away. • He learns how to read. • He doesn't trick anyone, he wants to be their friends.

5

Now that we've read and written our ideas in the Confirm column, let's check back to see which of our predictions actually happened. I'll put a shaded box around those predictions that came true and cross out those that didn't.

I = IMAGE	E = ELABORATE	**P = PREDICT**	C = CONFIRM
• Scary • big hairy • chases people • big teeth • hides in bushes • black eyes • drooling • Other animals are afraid • Night • Howling • Full moon • Chases animals	• I see a big black ferocious wolf showing its teeth • He is growling and licking his lips, as he corners a child • He is hungry and pacing back and forth • He is about to pounce on someone • He wants to eat the pigs. • Hunters will probably kill him • He is running in the snow with a pack of friends in the moonlight.	• He is not a real wolf, just a storybook wolf, I don't think he is going to eat anyone. • ~~He looks like Gunnywolf, maybe he'll sing songs.~~ • I think he is going to read to the animals instead of eating them. • After he reads, everyone will be happy. • He is not going to be mean at all. • ~~Maybe he will trick the animals by pretending to be nice and then eat them.~~	• He looks like a wolf, but he goes to school. • He starts off being mean. • He tries to scare the animals by howling and jumping. • Everyone is happy at the end. • Only the chickens and rabbits run away. • He learns how to read. • He doesn't trick anyone, he wants to be their friends.

Survey, Question, Read, Recite, Review (SQ3R)

STRATEGY 3:

Survey, Question, Read, Recite, Review (SQ3R)

By asking students to first survey text, then write questions, read to answer their questions, and finally review their answers, SQ3R demands comprehension monitoring before, during and after reading.

Step-by-Step

1. Teacher selects text, then models the SQ3R strategy on the overhead (see storyboard #1).
   a. **Survey:** He reads the headings, skims the introductory and summary paragraphs, and previews charts, diagrams and pictures (see storyboard #2).
   b. **Question:** Based on the title, the teacher thinks of, then writes, a question. Next, he reads each heading and thinks of and writes a question (see story-board #3).
   c. **Read:** The teacher reads the passage looking for the answers to his questions.
   d. **Recite:** He answers his questions.
   e. **Review:** After answering all questions, the teacher tests his comprehension by covering up the answers to see if he can remember them. If he can't, he re-reads the section (see storyboard #4).
2. The teacher assigns students to pairs and has them work through the strategy together.
3. The teacher holds students' accountable for what they learned by constructing a short quiz (see storyboard #5).

1

Today we are going to read about living, nonliving, and once living things. To help us understand what we read, we'll be using a strategy called Survey, Question, Read, Recite, Review, or SQ3R for short. I've made a poster to remind us of what to do for each of these processes.

SQ3R Chart

Survey - Skim the introductory and summary paragraphs and preview the pictures, diagrams and headings.
Question - Write questions after reading the title and each heading.
Read - Read the text.
Recite - Answer your questions.
Review - Study your questions by covering the answers. If you can't remember an answer, re-read that part.

Survey, Question, Read, Recite, Review (SQ3R)

2

Let's learn how to use this strategy together. I've placed the first two pages of the text we are going to read on the overhead. My first step is to SURVEY. So, I'll highlight and read the title, headings, and look at the pictures on the first page. Now you highlight the headings and survey the pictures on page two.

Dead or Alive

Look closely at the picture to the left. Notice that the rabbit is jumping through a field. We know this rabbit is alive, but how can we prove it? Beneath the rabbit is a picture of flowers. Are flowers living things? How do you know?

Characteristics & Examples of Living Things

- Reproduce
- Grow
- Move
- Breathe
- Eat
- Make waste

Now that you know the characteristics of living things, coming up with example is easier. Below is a list of examples of living things:

- Animals
- Plants
- Insects
- Birds
- Snails
- Worms

Nonliving Things

Nonliving things can move, but they do not grow, eat, breathe or make waste.

Characteristics of Nonliving Things

- Do not breathe
- Do not grow
- Do not eat
- Do not produce waste
- Do not reproduce or have parents

Some examples of nonliving things are:

- Rocks
- Crayons
- Wind
- Fire
- Metal

Most of the time it is easy to tell if something is living or nonliving. But sometimes things that were once living are now nonliving things.

After I SURVEY, my job is to ask QUESTIONS. I need to write a question for the TITLE and for each HEADING.

3

The title of the chapter is *Dead or Alive*. My question is "What makes something alive?" Can you think of another question? Share your question with a partner and compare your questions at your table. Let's think of a question for the first heading, *Characteristics and Examples of Living Things*.

Dead or Alive

Look closely at the picture to the right. Notice that the rabbit is jumping through a field. We know this rabbit is alive, but how can we prove it? Next to the rabbit is a picture of flowers. Are flowers living things? How do you know? How can your prove it?

QUESTIONS FOR TITLE
What makes something alive?
How do you know if something is dead?

Characteristics & Examples of Living Things

- Reproduce
- Grow
- Move
- Breathe
- Eat
- Make waste

QUESTIONS FOR HEADING
Can I give three examples of living things?
What characteristics make something living?

Now that you know the characteristics of living things, coming up with examples is easier. Below is a list of examples of living things:

- Animals
- Plants
- Insects
- Birds
- Snails
- Worms

Survey, Question, Read, Recite, Review (SQ3R)

4

So far, we've SURVEYED the text and developed QUESTIONS for the TITLE and one HEADING. I'm going to assign you to pairs, and your job is to write questions for each heading in the rest of the chapter. Then, you and your partner will read the chapter and answer your questions. Finally, you will review your questions and answers. I'm putting up the SQ3R Chart to remind you of what to do.

SQ3R

Survey - Skim the introductory and summary paragraphs and preview the pictures, diagrams and headings.
Question - Write questions after reading the title and each heading.
Read - Read the text.
Recite - Answer your questions.
Review - Study your questions by covering the answers. If you can't remember an answer, re-read that part.

5

Great work! Make sure you review and answer your questions because I developed a short quiz for this chapter to see how much you learned.

Reciprocal Teaching

Strategy 4:

Reciprocal Teaching

Reciprocal teaching relies on structured dialogue between teacher and students to teach students how to monitor their comprehension. Initially, the teacher directs the discussion and leads students in the use of four comprehension strategies. Then, as students learn the processes for interaction, they began to take on the teacher role. Each day, a new student leads his or her reading group by directing the discussion.

Step-by-Step

1. Teacher establishes reading groups.
2. Teacher introduces text students will read along with the four comprehension monitoring strategies that the group leader will use (see storyboard #2).
3. Prior to groups functioning independently, the teacher models the four comprehension jobs acting as the group leader for several weeks. She develops cue cards to teach students these jobs (see storyboards #4-7).
4. The four comprehension monitoring jobs are: Summarize, Generate Questions, Clarify and Predict. When the teacher leads the group, she models these jobs after every page (see storyboards #4-7).
   a. **Summarize** – First the teacher thinks aloud, asking the group what is the main idea, what big point does the author want us to remember.
   b. **Generate Questions** – Second, she poses questions about the page. As she models this behavior she teaches students how to identify the kind of information that is significant enough to provide the substance for a high-quality question.
   c. **Clarify** – Then, the teacher clarifies confusing parts or words that may be difficult to understand.
   d. **Predict** – Finally, the teacher makes a prediction, and asks for predictions from other group members.
5. To teach students how to engage in these four processes, the teacher clearly verbalizes her thinking and her expectations. And, each day the teacher designates more and more leadership responsibility to students.
6. When students can demonstrate that they can use these strategies and lead their own group discussion, the teacher shifts her role to facilitator and monitors several groups simultaneously (see storyboard #8).

Reciprocal Teaching

1

Isn't it more fun to talk about what you read with friends, instead of reading a book alone? Well, this year, when you read books, we are going to work on a strategy where you read in groups and each time you read, a different person will get to be the discussion leader.

2

Every time your group meets, you will take turns reading aloud. One person from your group is going to be the discussion leader, and that person is going to lead you in four comprehension monitoring strategies. I've made a poster of these strategies. Let's discuss them.

Reciprocal Teaching Leader Guide

Summarize – Stop after every page and state the big idea.

Generate Questions – Ask questions that make readers think.

Clarify – If the text is confusing or words are difficult, explain them or get help from others or the dictionary.

Predict – After every page, make a prediction. Write it down and check to see if it happens.

3

For the first few weeks groups will meet with me, and I'll be the group leader. I'm going to Summarize, Generate Questions, Clarify, and Predict. Then, as you learn these strategies, I'll pick a new group leader each day, and that person will lead the discussion while I watch, listen and coach.

4

To help the group leader remember these four comprehension monitoring strategies, I made cue cards. Each cue card defines the strategy and the job for the group leader. The first cue card is **Summarize.**

Summarize

The man in the picture is holding a machete and cutting through the brush to clear a path. A good summary cuts through all the details and just gives the big ideas.

Job: Stop after every page and summarize it in three sentences or less.

Reciprocal Teaching

5

GENERATE QUESTIONS

Question Words
Who
What
Why
Where
How
When

Generate Questions
Asking questions helps readers focus on the text and clear up things they may not understand.

Job: Use the *Question Words* on this card to ask your group questions after every page. Encourage your group members to ask questions as well.

6

CLARIFY

Clarify
If the text is confusing or words are not familiar, it can make understanding difficult.

Job: Write down words or phrases that are confusing. When a reader stops, explain these words, or get help from others or the dictionary.

7

PREDICT

Predict
Predicting what is going to happen next in a story gives your group a purpose for reading.

Job: Before reading each page, ask your group to discuss and make predictions. Write down one of the predictions and check to see if it actually happened.

8

The point of *Reciprocal Teaching* is for you all to monitor your comprehension by having meaningful discussions about the book you read. So, the goal is for you to become the teacher and use these strategies independently.

References

Brown, A.L. & Palincsar, A.S. (1985). *Reciprocal teaching of comprehension strategies: A natural history of one program for enhancing learning.* Technical Report No. 334, Center for the Study of Reading. Illinois University, Urbana, IL.

De La Paz, S. (1999). Self-regulated strategy instruction in regular education settings: Improving outcomes for students with and without learning disabilities. *Learning Disabilities Research and Practice, 14*, 92-118.

Pressley, M. & Wharton-McDonald, R. (1997). Skilled comprehension and its development through instruction. *School Psychology Review, 26*, 279-304.

Robinson, F.P. (1970). *Effective study (4th ed.)*. New York: Harper & Row.

Rosenshine, B. & Meister, C. (1994). Reciprocal teaching: A review of the research. *Review of Educational Research, 64*, 479-530.

Wood, K.D. & Endres, C. (2004). Motivating student interest with the imagine, elaborate, predict, and confirm (IEPC) strategy. *Reading Teacher, 58*, 346-357.

Question Answering

6

1 Definition

Most students answer questions only after reading, however, answering questions during reading requires that students attend to the text throughout the entire reading experience.

2 Chapter Preview

In this chapter we present

- four research-based question answering strategies with lesson storyboards.
- one video of a master teacher demonstrating the *Question Answer Relationship* (QARs) strategy.

3 Research

Question answering is most effective when students answer questions during and after reading and receive immediate feedback on their performance. Research on the four question answering strategies described in this chapter shows that teachers who implement these approaches produce students who comprehend 15 to 36 percent more on standardized reading assessments.

Notes

Question Answer Relationships

Strategy 1:

Question Answer Relationships (QARs)

The big idea behind the Question Answer Relationships (QARs) strategy is that there are essentially three types of comprehension questions (i.e., fact, integrate, inference). If students can identify the question type, they will be more likely to produce an appropriate answer.

Step-by-Step

1. Inform students that there are three different types of comprehension questions.
2. Create a QARs Chart and student Cue Cards (see storyboard #1).
3. Model how to use the QARs strategy (see storyboards #4-7) by:
   a. Selecting a short passage and developing three QARs comprehension questions.
   b. Placing the passage on an overhead projector and reading it aloud.
   c. Classifying each QARs question as a Green Light, Yellow Light, or Red Light question.
   d. Requiring students to answer each QAR.
   e. Repeating this process with another short passage.
4. Assign students a passage to read either individually or in small groups. Make sure you have prepared QARs questions for students to identify and answer.
5. Instruct students to use their QAR Cue Cards to classify, then answer each question (see storyboard #8).

Have you ever had to answer a question after you read and had a hard time figuring out what to write? Today you are going to learn a strategy to help you identify different types of comprehension questions so that you can answer them correctly. The strategy is called *Question Answer Relationships* or QARs.

RED LIGHT QUESTIONS
Stop and think because the answer cannot be found only in the text.

YELLOW LIGHT QUESTIONS
Slow down and search. You need to look in more than one place to put together your answer.

GREEN LIGHT QUESTIONS
Go and find the answer in one part of the text.

2

When you use the QARs strategy, the first thing you do is read. Then, you classify each question at the end of the selection. After you classify each question, you answer it. Let's look at our QARs Poster to help us classify questions.

RED LIGHT QUESTIONS
Stop and think because the answer cannot be found only in the text.

YELLOW LIGHT QUESTIONS
Slow down and search. You need to look in more than one place to put together your answer.

GREEN LIGHT QUESTIONS
Go and find the answer in one part of the text.

Question Answer Relationships

3

Green Light means GO. *Green Light Questions* have answers you can go and find in the text. Yellow Light means SLOW DOWN. For *Yellow Light Questions* you need to look in more than one place for the answer. *Red Light* means STOP. These questions don't have answers you can find in the text; you have to stop, think, and use your knowledge.

RED LIGHT QUESTIONS
Stop and think because the answer cannot be found only in the text.

YELLOW LIGHT QUESTIONS
Slow down and search. You need to look in more than one place in the text to put together your answer.

GREEN LIGHT QUESTIONS
Go and find the answer in one part of the text.

4

On the overhead is a passage about an intelligent animal, Siti, an orangutan. I'm going to read the text.

Siti the Orangutan

Safe in a sanctuary after being rescued from people who kept her illegally as a pet, Siti the orangutan struggled to crack open a coconut. Unable to open it, Siti approached a sanctuary worker and handed it to him. The worker just handed it back because he was trying to let Siti learn how to survive in the forest. Siti poked at the coconut with a stick, then gave it back to him. Again, the worker played dumb and handed it back.

"Siti must have decided the man was stupid," says psychologist Anne Russon, who was watching. Siti picked up another stick and hacked at the coconut as one would with a long knife. She showed the worker what she wanted him to do—something she'd seen him do many times. "Siti herself had never opened a coconut," says Russon. "Yet she had learned how it was done, just by watching."

QARs Cue Card

RED LIGHT QUESTIONS
Stop and think

YELLOW LIGHT QUESTIONS
Slow down and search

GREEN LIGHT QUESTIONS
Go and find the answer

5

Here are some questions about this passage. Let's decide if they are *Green Light, Yellow Light* or *Red Light Questions* together.

Questions	QARs Classification
1. What was the sanctuary worker's reason for handing the coconut back to Siti?	*This is a Green Light Question. With a partner underline where in the text you can find the answer.*
2. Why did Siti think the sanctuary worker was stupid?	*Can the answer for this question be found in the text? Do you have to look in more than one place?*
3. Why do you think being able to imitate is a sign of intelligence?	*This is a Red Light Question. In your table groups, tell me why.*

QARs Cue Card

RED LIGHT QUESTIONS
Stop and think

YELLOW LIGHT QUESTIONS
Slow down and search

GREEN LIGHT QUESTIONS
Go and find the answer

6

Let's do another example together. This selection is about elephant intelligence. Let's read it together. This time you're going to decide if the questions are Green, Yellow, or Red before you answer them.

Elephant Intelligence

A baby elephant stumbled into a dried-up mud hole in Amboseli National Park in Kenya, Africa. Luckily the calf didn't get hurt, but it was too little to scramble out. The elephant's mother ran into the hole after her baby. Then she bellowed.

Two relatives heard the commotion and rushed over to help. First, they sized up the situation. It wasn't a terribly deep hole, but the sides were steep. Then, they climbed into the pit. As the elephants dug out one side of the hole with their tusks and feet, a ramp was formed by the loosened dirt.

The minute they finished, the mother pushed her calf up the incline. The elephants seemed to plan ahead, imagining how a ramp would work to save the baby. Even Einstein would have been impressed.

QARs Cue Card

RED LIGHT QUESTIONS
Stop and think

YELLOW LIGHT QUESTIONS
Slow down and search

GREEN LIGHT QUESTIONS
Go and find the answer

Question Answer Relationships

7

Here are the questions. Decide at your tables if they are *Green, Yellow,* or *Red Light Questions,* and then answer them.

Questions	QARs Classification
1. Give and defend two reasons why, "even Einstein would have been impressed' by these elephant problem solvers.	*IF YOU SAID YELLOW LIGHT AND YOUR ANSWER WAS WORKED TOGETHER, DUG HOLE, OR MADE A RAMP, YOU ARE RIGHT.*
2. What did the mother elephant do after her baby fell into the hole?	*Look at your QARs Cue Card. Can the answer be found in the text in one place? THIS IS A GREEN LIGHT QUESTION.*
3. What made these elephants' problem solving behaviors human-like?	*THIS IS A RED LIGHT QUESTION. YOU NEED TO THINK ABOUT HUMAN PROBLEM SOLVING, AND HOW THE ELEPHANTS ACTED IN HUMAN WAYS.*

8

On your desk are passages about different intelligent animals. Each passage is followed by 2 to 4 questions. With a partner, read about the animal, then read the questions. Before you answer a question, classify it as Green, Yellow, or Red. After you classify each question, discuss the answer and write it in the space provided.

QARs Poster

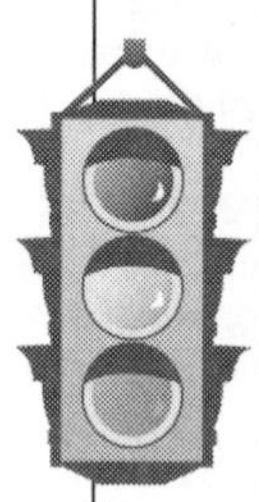

RED LIGHT QUESTIONS
Stop and think because the answer cannot be found only in the text.

YELLOW LIGHT QUESTIONS
Slow down and search. You need to look in more than one place to put together your answer.

GREEN LIGHT QUESTIONS
Go and find the answer in one part of the text.

Passage Skeletons

STRATEGY 2:

Passage Skeletons

Passage Skeletons visually represent and organize information teachers want students to extract from the text. Students, by filling in their *Passage Skeletons* while they read, interact with text throughout their reading experience.

Studies have demonstrated that students that use *Passage Skeletons* record 71percent more important ideas and concepts than students not instructed to use this strategy.

Step-by-Step

1. Inform students that they will read a selection and while they read, they will fill in their *Passage Skeletons* (see storyboards #2-3).
2. Explain that a *Passage Skeleton* presents an outline of the text with space for students to fill in the details and important ideas.
3. What's critical when a teacher designs *Passage Skeletons* is that she identifies the facts, concepts, and relationships she wants students to understand and record.
4. Make sure to provide consistent symbols for student contributions (e.g., blank lines, bullets, numbered sequences, etc.) so that students know where and how much detail their answers should include (see storyboards #2 and #3).
5. *Passage Skeletons* should not require students to write too much, but they should also not exclusively require filling in blanks.

1

For social studies we are going to read about the Navajo Indians. As you read, you are going to be using a comprehension strategy called *Passage Skeletons.*

2

Here is the first page of your *Passage Skeleton.* The first paragraph in our text about the Navajo discusses the region where they lived. Your *Passage Skeleton* asks you to draw a circle around that region.

The Navajo Passage Skeleton

On the map draw a circle around where the Navajo lived before the European invasion.

Before the Civil War the number of Navajo Indians was ____________. The Navajo lived in the following four states:
1. **Arizona**
2.
3.
4.

Early on, the Navajo were a nomadic people. What did they hunt? Which foods did they collect?______________________________

In the 1600s the Spaniards taught the Navajo to herd what type of animals and grow which type of vegetable?________________
____

Next, the Passage Skeleton asks about what the Navajo hunted and the foods they gathered. There is a short space for you to answer.

Then, you'll read about what the Navajo learned from the Spaniards. Again, fill in the answer in the Skeleton.

Passage Skeletons

3

The second page of your *Passage Skeleton* outlines big ideas for you to answer about Navajo housing and ceremonies.

The Navajo Passage Skeleton

The Navajo lived in houses called Hogans. There are two types of Hogans, male and female. What things occur in the male hogan?

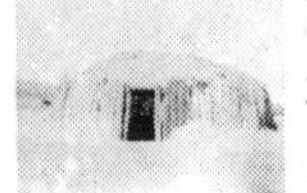

1. ____________________
2. ____________________
3. ____________________

What things occur in the female hogan?

1. ____________________
2. ____________________
3. ____________________

Navajo people have many different types of ceremonies: Define the following ceremonies.

POW WOW____________________

YEIBECHEI DANCE____________________

FIRE DANCE ____________________

We are looking for three things male and female hogans are used for.

As you read about the Navajo ceremonies, define these three in the space provided.

4

When you complete your reading and *Passage Skeleton* compare your answers with one person at your table. Then, come up to the board and write two questions you have about what you read. We'll discuss your *Passage Skeleton* answers and questions at the end of the period.

Whiteboard

Pair Questions

Is the Navajo language still used?

Why do Navajo people live so far apart?

Where did Navajo people originally come from?

What's so special about Canyon De Shelly?

How did the Navajo come to be such excellent weavers?

How do the weavers get the color for their rugs?

Why are so many rocks in the Navajo region red?

Reading Guides

STRATEGY 3:

Reading Guides

Reading Guides identify where in the text students should focus to find answers to comprehension questions. Unlike most textbooks that list questions for students to answer after they read, *Reading Guides* provide questions for students to answer during reading.

Step-by-Step

1. Teacher reads text and develops a *Reading Guide* by creating an equal number of questions that students will answer from the beginning, middle, and end of the text (see storyboard #1).
2. Next to each *Reading Guide* question, the teacher lists the page and paragraph number where students can find the answer.
3. Students read the *Reading Guide* questions first, and then read the text looking for answers (see storyboards #2-3).
4. After every page, students check to see if a *Reading Guide* question relates to that page (see storyboard #4)

1

Today we are going to read a Library of Congress selection titled *Lincoln's Gettysburg Address*. To help you understand what you read, we'll be using *Reading Guides*. A *Reading Guide* has a set of questions followed by parentheses that tell you on which page and in which paragraph you can find information to help you answer the question.

Reading Guide for Lincoln's Gettysburg Address

1. Why did Lincoln go to Gettysburg? **(Page 1, paragraph 1)**
2. How did Wills get the land for the cemetery? **(Page 1, paragraph 3)**
3. What ideas were central to Lincoln's address? **(Page 1, paragraph 5)**
4. How many years is four score and seven years? **(Page 2, paragraph 1)**

2

Let's read the first question. *Why did Lincoln go to Gettysburg?* On what page and paragraph can we find the information to help us answer this? That's right, page 1 paragraph 1. I'll read the first paragraph on page 1, and then let's discuss the answer together.

Reading Guide for Lincoln's Gettysburg Address

1. Why did Lincoln go to Gettysburg? **(Page 1, paragraph 1)**

Text excerpted from the Library of Congress, *The Gettysburg Address*

On November 2, 1863, several months after the battle of Gettysburg, David Wills invited President Lincoln to make a "few appropriate remarks" at the consecration of a cemetery for the Union war dead.

Can we find the answer to question 1 in the first paragraph? Sure, it says Lincoln went to Gettysburg to bless a cemetery created to bury the Union soldiers who died on the Gettysburg battlefield.

Reading Guides

3

Let's try question 2 together before you work on your own. On what page and paragraph can we find the information to answer question 2? That's right, page 1, paragraph 3.

Reading Guide For Lincoln's Gettysburg Address

2. How did Wills get the land for the cemetery?
   (Page 1, paragraph 3)

Text excerpted from the Library of Congress, The Gettysburg Address

1. On November 2, 1863, several months after the battle of Gettysburg, David Wills invited President Lincoln to make a "few appropriate remarks" at the consecration of a cemetery for the Union war dead.

2. In early July, Pennsylvania governor Andrew Curtin had charged Wills, a successful local citizen and judge, with cleaning up the horrible aftermath of the battle (where 28,063 Confederates and 23,049 Union soldiers were killed or wounded). Wounded soldiers were crammed into every available building, and thousands of swollen dead were strewn among hundreds of bloated dead horses.

3. With the approval of the governor and the eighteen states whose sons were among the dead, Wills quickly acquired seventeen acres for the national cemetery and had the Germantown landscape architect, William Saunders, draw up a plan. Burial began not long after.

We see that the governor and eighteen states approved the purchase of the Gettysburg land for a national cemetery.

4

To use a *Reading Guide,* you first read the questions and underline what page and paragraph information can be found to help you answer. Next, you read one page at a time. Then, you answer the questions for that page.

Reading Guide for Lincoln's Gettysburg Address

1. Why did Lincoln go to Gettysburg?
   (Page 1, paragraph 1)

2. How did Wills get the land for the cemetery?
   (Page 1, paragraph 3)

3. What ideas were central to Lincoln's address?
   (Page 1, paragraph 5)

4. How many years is four score and seven years?
   (Page 2 paragraph 1)

Reading Guides

STRATEGY 4:

Class-Wide Peer Tutoring

Class Wide Peer Tutoring (CWPT) has produced long lasting reading comprehension gains of 26 to 44 percent. By requiring students to answer comprehension questions under the supervision of a peer, this strategy increases the amount of feedback students receive, and ensures that help is immediate, specific, and correct.

Step-by-Step

1. Teacher introduces text that tutor and tutee will read.
2. Teacher writes 10 questions for students to answer (i.e., 3 questions for the beginning, 4 for the middle, and 3 for the end of the text).
3. Teacher assigns tutor-tutee partners.
4. Teacher models tutor behaviors by:
   a) Placing a paragraph and question on the overhead projector.
   b) Reading the paragraph and role-playing the tutor and tutee interaction (e.g., tutor provides cues as to where to find the answer; tutor prompts tutee to find supporting details; tutor provides feedback on why an answer is or is not correct).
   c) Teacher places a second paragraph and question on the overhead projector, and role plays again.
5. Getting tutors to give high-quality feedback, and not just the answers, will take several instances of modeling along with careful monitoring and feedback to tutors while they work on this strategy.
6. Teacher passes out one half of the text and 5 questions to the tutee and the answer sheet for those 5 questions to the tutor.
7. Teacher reminds students to stop at the end of each page and review the questions to see which questions can be answered.
8. Tutor answer sheet has information about where to locate the answers and the answer for each of the 5 questions.
9. After reading half of the text and answering 5 questions, tutor and tutee switch roles. The teacher distributes the answer sheets to the new tutor and the second half of text and questions to the new tutee.
10. To close the lesson, the teacher reviews some of the more difficult questions with the whole class. He also tells pairs to turn in their written answers and explains that they will be graded based on the pair's performance.

References

Greenwood, C. R (1993). Achievement, placement, and services: Middle school benefits of class-wide peer tutoring used at the elementary school. *School Psychology Review, 22,* 497-516.

Greenwood, C.R. (1991). Longitudinal analysis of time, engagement and achievement in at risk versus non-risk students. *Exceptional Children, 57,* 521-535.

Greenwood, C.R., Delquadri, J. & Hall, R.V. (1989). Longitudinal effects of class-wide peer tutoring. *Journal of Educational Psychology, 81,* 371-383.

Horton, S.V. & Lovitt, T.C. (1989). Using study guides with three classifications of secondary students. *The Journal of Special Education, 22,* 447-462.

Horton, S.V., Lovitt, T.C. & Christensen, C.C. (1991). Matching three classifications of secondary students to three different levels of study guides. *Journal of Learning Disabilities, 24,* 518-529.

Kiewra, K.A., Mayer, R.E., Christensen, M., Kim, S. & Risch, N. (1991). Effects of repetition on recall and note taking: Strategies from learning from lectures. *Journal of Educational Psychology, 83,* 120-123.

Lawrence, K.M. (2002). Red light, green light, 1-2-3: Tasks to prepare for standardized tests. *The Reading Teacher, 55,* 525-528.

Raphael, T.E. & Wonnacott, C.A. (1985). Heightening fourth grade students' sensitivity to sources of information for answering comprehension questions. *Reading Research Quarterly, 20,* 282-296.

Multi-Strategy Instruction

7

1 Definition

When professor Michael Pressley studied expert readers, he found that they used more than one comprehension strategy at a time. Expert readers:
(1) generate and answer questions;
(2) relate what they read to what they know;
(3) make predictions;
(4) summarize;
(5) visualize;
(6) elaborate, organize, re-read, etc.

2 Chapter Preview

In this chapter we present

- four strategies and visual lesson storyboards that promote the use of multiple comprehension strategies.
- two videos of master teachers teaching the *Question, Summarize, Clarify* strategy and *Literature Circles*.

3 Research

Students taught a variety of comprehension strategies along with when, how, and where to use them outperform students in traditional reading instruction by 40 to 50 percent. Moreover, the teaching of multiple comprehension strategies increases students' willingness to read complex texts and discover their underlying meanings.

Notes

Strategy 1:

POSSE

The POSSE strategy relies on cooperative groups to implement five research-based comprehension strategies.

POSSE
P = PREDICT
O = ORGANIZE
S = SEARCH
S = SUMMARIZE
E = EVALUATE

Step-by-Step

1. The teacher selects the text that students will read and places them in groups of four.
2. He distributes a POSSE strategy sheet to each student (see storyboard #3).
3. On a class POSSE sheet, the teacher models how to Predict, Organize, Search, and Summarize (see storyboards #4-8).
   a. First, the teacher reads the text's title and shows students some of the pictures and diagrams. He asks groups to put their heads together and make three predictions on their POSSE sheet. The teacher then writes some of those predictions on the class POSSE chart.
   b. Next, the teacher asks groups to use their predictions to think of and write two questions about the text. The teacher first verbalizes his question, and then solicits questions from groups and writes them on the class POSSE sheet (see storyboard #5).
   c. Then, the teacher reads a couple paragraphs aloud, stops, and has the class discuss the main idea and supporting details. The teacher writes the main idea and supporting details for the paragraphs in the organize/search/summrize section of the class POSSE sheet (see storyboard #7).
4. The teacher assigns students to continue reading in groups and to identify main ideas and supporting details by filling in the organize/search/summarize section of their POSSE sheet.
5. When students complete the organize/search/summarize section of their POSSE sheets, the teacher engages the class in a discussion where groups compare their predictions to what they learned (see storyboard #9).

POSSE

1

In social studies we've been learning about the individuals and groups responsible for the founding of the American colonies. Last week we studied the Massachusetts colony led by John Winthrop.

Today we're going to read about William Penn, who founded Pennsylvania. William Penn was America's first great champion for liberty and peace.

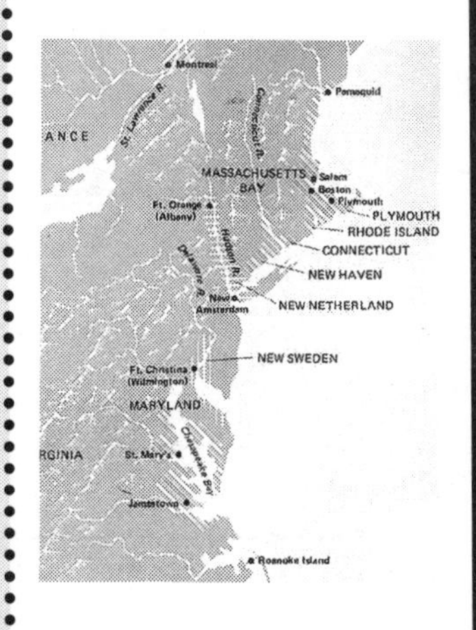

2

To help us understand why William Penn founded Pennsylvania and what made him such a great American, we'll use a comprehension strategy called POSSE. On the wall is a POSSE poster. You'll use this poster along with the POSSE strategy sheet to help you understand and remember what you read. POSSE stands for:

POSSE

P = PREDICT

O = ORGANIZE

S = SEARCH

S = SUMMARIZE

E = EVALUATE

3

I'm going to put you into POSSE's of four students. Your group will be responsible for Predicting, Organizing, Searching, Summarizing and Evaluating what you read using the POSSE strategy sheet.

POSSE Strategy Sheet

Predict some of the ideas you may find in the text.
1.____________________
2.____________________
3.____________________
4.____________________
5.____________________

Write two questions you have about the text.
1.____________________
2.____________________

Topic

Main Idea — Details

Main Idea — Details

Main Idea — Details

Main Idea — Details

Main Idea — Details

Compare your organizer to your predictions. What did you learn that was new?

____

Answer your questions.

____

POSSE

4

Let me show you how to use the POSSE strategy sheet. Before your group reads, put your heads together and predict what you think you'll learn about William Penn. Then, write two questions you want the text to answer.

Predict some of the ideas you may find in the text.
1.____
2.____
3.____
4.____
5.____

Write two questions you have about the text.
1.____
2.____

POSSE Strategy Sheet

Topic → Main Idea (×5), each with Details ____

Compare your organizer to your predictions. What did you learn that was new?
____

Answer your questions.
____

5

When your group predicts, it's a good idea to read the title, the first paragraph, and skim the headings. Each of you has the article on William Penn, so take a minute and skim it. Then, put your heads together and predict what the text may be about. Write at least 3 predictions in the Predict part of the POSSE strategy sheet.

William Penn, America's First Great Champion for Liberty and Peace

William Penn was the first great hero of American liberty. During the late seventeenth century, when Protestants persecuted Catholics, Catholics persecuted Protestants, and both persecuted Quakers and Jews, Penn established an American sanctuary which protected freedom of conscience. Almost everywhere else, colonists stole land from the Indians, but Penn traveled unarmed among the Indians and negotiated peaceful purchases. He insisted that women deserved equal rights with men. He gave Pennsylvania a written constitution which limited the power of government, provided a humane penal code, and guaranteed many fundamental liberties.

Predict some of the ideas you may find in the text.

1. *Champion for liberty*
2. *Helped women's rights*
3. *Freedom of religion*

Write two questions you have about the text.

1. *How did William Penn get the land for Pennsylvania?*
2. *Who influenced William Penn's ideas about government?*

After your group has made its predictions, think of and write two questions you want the text to answer.

POSSE

6

Let's record some of your predictions and questions on the class POSSE strategy sheet.

Predict some of the ideas you may find in the text.

1. *Champion for liberty*
2. *Helped women's rights*
3. *Freedom of religion*

Write two questions you have about the text.

1. *How did William Penn get the land for Pennsylvania?*
2. *Who influenced William Penn's ideas about government?*

POSSE Strategy Sheet

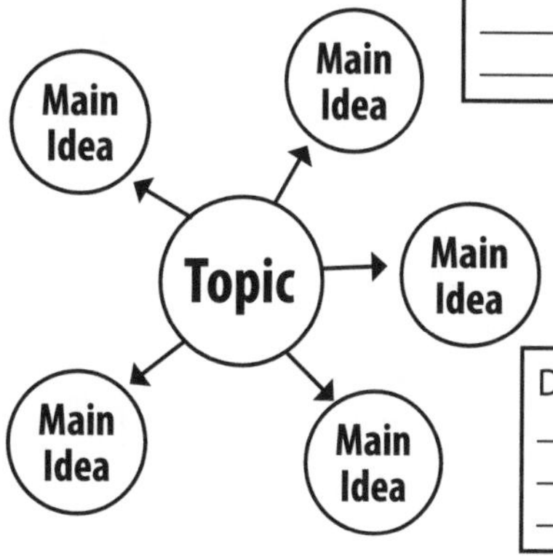

Details

______

Details

______

Details

______

Details

______

Details

______

Compare your organizer to your predictions. What did you learn that was new?

______

Answer your questions.

______

7

In your groups, read the first page about William Penn. Search for two main ideas, and write each in a main idea bubble in the organizer. Then, write some details for each of these ideas. When you finish, we'll have a discussion, and I'll write two main ideas and details in my organizer.

William Penn: America's First Great Champion . . .
For the first time in modem history, a large society offered equal rights to people of different races and religions. Penn's dramatic example caused quite a stir in Europe. The French philosopher Voltaire, a champion of religious toleration, offered lavish praise. "William Penn might, with reason, boast of having brought down upon earth the Golden Age, which in all probability, never had any real existence but in his dominions."

Penn was the only person who made major contributions to liberty in both the New World and the Old World. Before he conceived the idea of Pennsylvania, he became the leading defender of religious toleration in England. He was imprisoned six times for speaking out courageously. While in prison, he wrote one pamphlet after another, which gave Quakers a literature and attacked intolerance. He alone proved capable of challenging oppressive government policies in court--one of his cases helped secure the right to trial by jury. Penn used his diplomatic skills and family connections to get large numbers of Quakers out of jail.

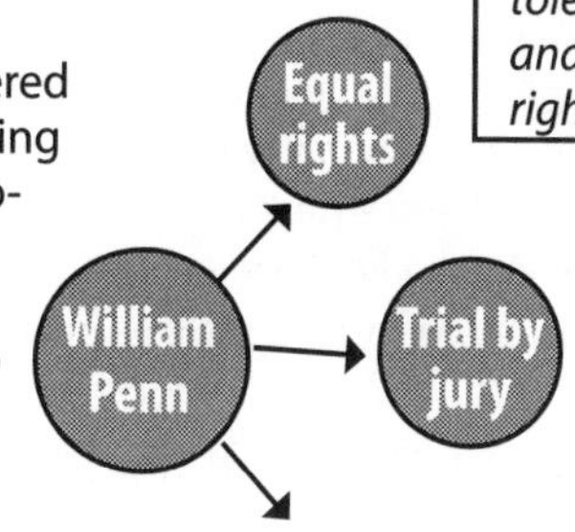

Details
Penn defended religious tolerance, race tolerance and promoted equal rights.

Details
Penn challenged England's legal policies and helped secure the right to trial by jury.

Details

______

POSSE

8

Now read the rest of the text and complete the Organize, Search, and Summarize tasks (i.e., identifying the main ideas and accompanying details in the graphic organizer section). When you finish, compare your organizer to your predictions and write something new your group learned.

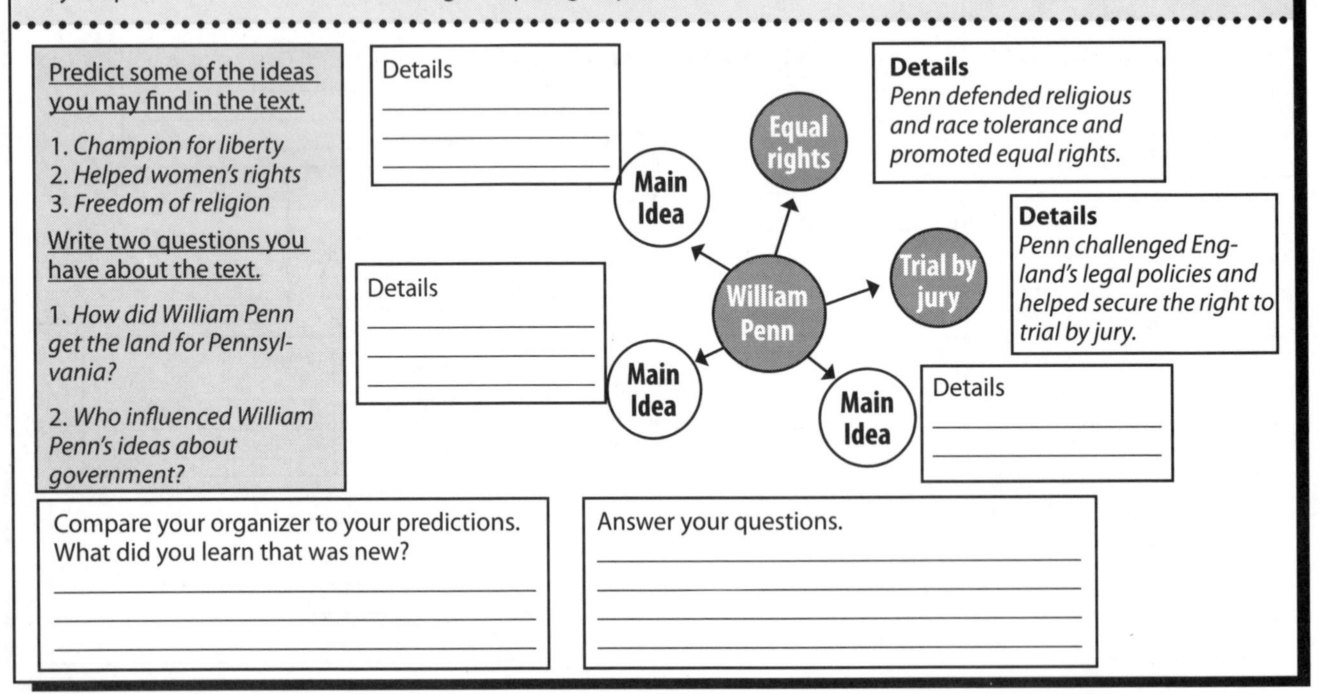

Compare your organizer to your predictions. What did you learn that was new?

Answer your questions.

9

Let's share some of our comparisons. Let's also share some of the new ideas we learned about William Penn.

Compare your organizer to your predictions. What did you learn that was new?

- We knew Penn was for liberty, but we didn't know that he was a lawyer. He was also a Quaker and he helped get Quakers out of jail.
- Even though we predicted Penn was for people's rights, we read that he owned slaves. This doesn't seem right since he was so devoted to individual freedom.
- We discovered that Pennsylvania was not named after Penn, but his dad. We also learned that Philadelphia means city of brotherly love in Greek.
- To help women's rights, Penn encouraged women to get an education and speak out as men did.
- As governor, Penn provided for secure private property, free enterprise, a free press, trial by jury, and religious tolerance.
- Penn's religious tolerance and peace policies led Pennsylvania to become America's first cultural melting pot.
- In England there were 200 offenses where someone could get the death penalty. In Pennsylvania, just two--murder and treason.

Question, Summarize, Clarify

Strategy 2:

Question, Summarize, Clarify

Questioning, summarizing and clarifying vocabulary are three comprehension strategies, each with substantial research support. Combining these three strategies into one can increase the learning benefits threefold.

Step-by-Step

1. Prior to reading, provide each student with a small stack of Post-it Notes.
2. Design a three-column T-Chart organizer labeled: Question, Summarize, and Clarify (see storyboard #4).
3. Inform students that as they read, they will generate questions, write page summaries, and record words they do not understand on Post-it Notes (see storyboard #5).
4. Model to students how they will perform each of these actions by placing the first page of the assigned text on an overhead projector and reading it aloud (see storyboards #6-8).
    a. Stop after each paragraph, think aloud, and write down a question on a Post-it.
    b. When you encounter a word you are not sure of, write the word on a clarify Post-it Note.
    c. After you finish reading the page, write a two-sentence summary on a Post-it Note.
5. After modeling each of the three parts of this strategy, assign students to read and record (questions, summaries, and word clarifications) in pairs (see storyboard #9).

1

Today, we'll begin our study of ancient Egypt by reading about and discussing the main features of Egyptian art and architecture. Before we read, let's preview some of the pictures in the article.

2

Egyptian architecture is famous for its pyramids. But did you know that Egyptian buildings also relied heavily on columns. In all there were 11 different column designs.

Question, Summarize, Clarify

3

When you look at the sculptures that adorned palaces and tombs, notice the simplicity, the attention to the basic human form, and the solemn faces. As we will read, many of these artistic elements were central to the idea of passing on to the afterlife.

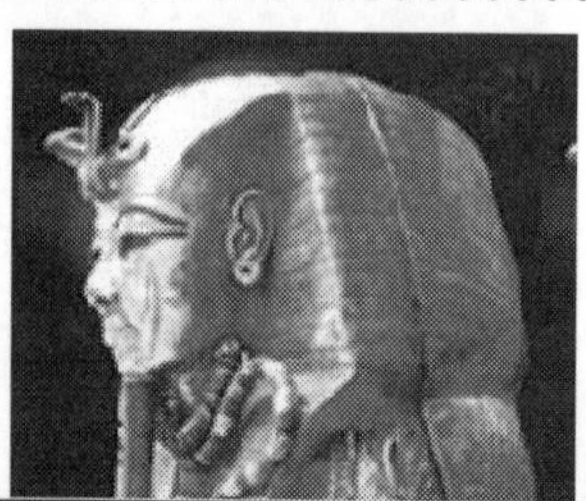

4

Now that we've previewed some pictures of Egyptian art and architecture, we are going to read an article about it. To help us understand the decisions the architects and artists of Egypt made, we are going to use a comprehension strategy called Question, Summarize, and Clarify.

QSC Chart

Question	Summarize	Clarify

5

Let's put up the first page of the article on the overhead. Your job is to come up with a question after each paragraph, a summary for each page, and to write down words that you don't understand. When you finish reading each page, your Post-it Notes should look like this.

The king of Egypt was considered a divine being who held sway over the pyramids, and on his departure from this earth he would again ascend to the gods whence he had come. The pyramids soaring up to the sky would probably help him to make his ascent. In any case they would preserve his sacred body from decay. For the Egyptians believed that the body must be preserved if the soul is to live on in the beyond.

Question

"But it is not only these pyramids which tell of the role played by age-old beliefs in the story of art. The Egyptians held the belief that the preservation of the body was not enough. If the likeness of the king was also preserved, it was doubly sure that he would continue to exist forever. So they ordered sculptors to chisel the king's head out of hard, imperishable granite, and put it in the tomb where no one saw it, there to work its spell and to help his Soul to keep alive in and through the image. One Egyptian word for sculptor was actually 'He-who-keeps-alive.'

Clarify

Question

Some of these early portraits from the pyramid age, the fourth dynasty of the Old Kingdom, are among the most beautiful works of Egyptian art. There is a solemnity and simplicity about them, which one does not easily forget. One sees that the sculptor was not trying to flatter his sitter, or to preserve a fleeting expression. He was concerned only with essentials. Perhaps it is just because of this strict concentration on the basic forms of the human head that these portraits remain so impressive. This combination of geometric regularity and keen observation of nature is characteristic of all Egyptian art. We can study it best in the reliefs and paintings that adorned the walls of the tombs.

Question

Summary

6

I'm going to read the first paragraph, think of a question, and underline words that I don't know. Then, I'll write my question and clarification words on different Post-it Notes.

The king of Egypt was considered a divine being who held sway over the pyramids, and on his departure from this earth he would again ascend to the gods whence he had come. The pyramids soaring up to the sky would probably help him to make his ascent. In any case they would preserve his sacred body from decay. For the Egyptians believed that the body must be preserved if the soul is to live on in the beyond.

Question: Why did Egyptian kings build pyramids?

Clarify: divine, sway, ascend, whence, sacred

Question, Summarize, Clarify

7

Now I'll read the second paragraph. Notice that I am writing a question and words that I don't understand for this paragraph on Post-it Notes.

The king of Egypt was considered a divine being who held sway over the pyramids, and on his departure from this earth he would again ascend to the gods whence he had come. The pyramids soaring up to the sky would probably help him to make his ascent. In any case they would preserve his sacred body from decay. For the Egyptians believed that the body must be preserved if the soul is to live on in the beyond.

"But it is not only these pyramids which tell of the role played by age-old beliefs in the story of art. The Egyptians held the belief that the preservation of the body was not enough. If the likeness of the king was also preserved, it was doubly sure that he would continue to exist forever. So they ordered sculptors to chisel the king's head out of hard, imperishable granite, and put it in the tomb where no one saw it, there to work its spell and to help his Soul to keep alive in and through the image. One Egyptian word for sculptor was actually 'He-who-keeps-alive'.

Question:
Why did Egyptian kings build pyramids?

Clarify:
Divine
Sway
Ascend
Preservation
Preserved
Chisel
Imperishable

Question:
For what reason did Egyptian kings believe they needed to preserve their images through art?

8

Ok, I've developed my questions and clarifications after each paragraph for this page. I need to write a one or two sentence summary on a Post-it and write the page number so I know which page I summarized. When I complete each page, I have question Post-its, clarifying words Post-its and a summary Post-it.

The king of Egypt was considered a divine being who held sway over the pyramids, and on his departure from this earth he would again ascend to the gods whence he had come. The pyramids soaring up to the sky would probably help him to make his ascent. In any case they would preserve his sacred body from decay. For the Egyptians believed that the body must be preserved if the soul is to live on in the beyond.

"But it is not only these pyramids which tell of the role played by age-old beliefs in the story of art. The Egyptians held the belief that the preservation of the body was not enough. If the likeness of the king was also preserved, it was doubly sure that he would continue to exist forever. So they ordered sculptors to chisel the king's head out of hard, imperishable granite, and put it in the tomb where no one saw it, there to work its spell and to help his Soul to keep alive in and through the image. One Egyptian word for sculptor was actually 'He-who-keeps-alive'.

Some of these early portraits from the pyramid age, the fourth dynasty of the Old Kingdom, are among the most beautiful works of Egyptian art. There is a solemnity and simplicity about them, which one does not easily forget. One sees that the sculptor was not trying to flatter his sitter, or to preserve a fleeting expression. He was concerned only with essentials. Perhaps it is just because of this strict concentration on the basic forms of the human head that these portraits remain so impressive. This combination of geometric regularity and keen observation of nature is characteristic of all Egyptian art. We can study it best in the reliefs and paintings that adorned the walls of the tombs.

Question: Why did Egyptian kings build pyramids?

Question: For what reason did Egyptian kings believe they needed to preserve their images through art?

Clarify: Ascend, Preservation, Preserved, Chisel, Imperishable, Granite, Fleeting, Geometric regularity, Reliefs, Adorned

Question: Why didn't Egyptian artists want to make the King look beautiful?

Summary: The architecture of the pyramids and the sculptures and paintings within them served the purpose of helping the king's soul pass to the afterlife (page 1).

9

When you and your partner finish the article and complete all your Post-it Notes, place them under the correct category on your QSC Chart like this. Then answer your questions.

QSC Chart

Question	Summarize	Clarify
Question: Why did Egyptian kings build pyramids? **Question:** For what reason did Egyptian kings believe they needed to preserve their images through art? **Question:** Why didn't Egyptian artists want to make the King look beautiful?	**Summary:** The architecture of the pyramids and the sculptures and paintings within them served the purpose of helping the king's soul pass to the afterlife (page 1)	**Clarify:** Ascend Preservation Preserved Chisel Imperishable Granite Fleeting Geometric regularity Reliefs Adorned

10

After you've answered your questions, pick your best question, summary, and three clarification words. Then, come up and place these Post-it Notes on our class Chart so we can talk about them together.

I-Chart Example

STRATEGY 3:

I-Charts

I-Charts include the following comprehension strategies: question answering, question generation, summarizing, identifying interesting facts, and reading multiple texts on the same topic to widen one's perspective. Implementing I-Charts consists of three phases: Planning, Interacting, and Integrating.

Step-by-Step

1. **Planning**
   a. **Topic**. Teacher identifies the topic and reading materials by collecting three texts from textbooks, encyclopedias, trade books, magazines, newspapers, or the Internet. Teacher lists each text's bibliographic information (see example).
   b. **Questions**. Teacher writes four questions. These questions address the most significant ideas of the topic.
   c. **Facts**. In row 1, columns 6 and 7, the teacher creates headings that say *Interesting Facts* and *Student Questions*.
   d) **Summary**. In column 1, row 7, the teacher writes the heading *Summary*. The teacher produces a chart similar to the one in the example and distributes a photocopy to every student.
2. **Interacting**
   a. **Explore prior knowledge and beliefs**. Before assigning the reading, the teacher probes students' knowledge by asking them to respond to each question on their I-Chart in writing (see example).
   b. **Sharing interesting facts and questions**. Before reading, the teacher shares an interesting fact and asks students for other questions they have about the topic.
   c. **Read and record**. In pairs, students read the various sources, answer the questions, list interesting facts, and develop new questions (see example).
3. **Integrating**
   a. **Summarize**. In pairs, students generate summary statements for each question from the various sources.
   b. **Compare**. Using whole class discussion, the teacher guides students in comparing the summary statements with students' prior knowledge and beliefs.
   c. **Research**. For homework, in the new questions column, the teacher assigns students to research answers to one of their questions.
   d. **Report**. Students report back to the class their findings.

I-Chart Example

1	TOPIC Christopher Columbus	Question #1	Question #2	Question #3	Question #4	Interesting Facts	Student Questions
2		1. Why did he sail?	2. What did he find?	3. What things did he do when he got there?	4. How was Columbus regarded by others?		
3	**WHAT WE KNOW ABOUT COLUMBUS**	to prove the world was round	America	. . . not sure	he was a hero	He sailed in 1492 and was Spanish	Did he have a family?
4	Source 1 – Christopher Columbus, Man & Myth – Web site	He was trying to find a new route to the Indies.	He found friendly Indians, some gold, different islands.	He claimed the new land for Isabella and Ferdinand.	When he got back people regarded him as a great man.	He asked the king of Portugal for ships but was turned down.	What happened to his son?
5	Source 2 – Columbus, The World Book Encyclopedia 1979	To find riches and a shorter route to the Indies. He wanted to be famous to be known as a great explorer.	He found America.	He named the islands. He captured some Indians as slaves. He become governor.	He was a dreamy person. He had a lot of friends.	He had two sons not one, six brothers and a sister. He was born in Italy. He claimed his discovery was God's work.	What did Columbus do with the slaves he captured?
6	Source 3 - Where Do You Think You Are Going Christopher Columbus? Putnam and Sons, 1980	He liked to travel. He sought a big reward for finding a new route to the Indies.	He found Indians and some small hunks of gold.	He asked the Indians for directions to the Palace of Khan.	Before he went he was wealthy because he married a rich woman.	He sounded greedy in this book. He said he saw land first .	Was he really cruel to the Indians?
7	**SUMMARY**	To find a new route to the Indies. To find riches and become famous. He already knew the world was round.	He found America, islands, and some gold.	He claimed the new land for Spain. He named the islands. He took some Indians back as slaves. He became governor.	After he sailed he was famous and a hero. He seemed greedy. Everyone forgot about him after a while.	He claimed he was doing God's work. His family supported him. He tried to get money for his voyage from lots of people. He was born an Italian.	Find out more about his family, his treatment of Indians, and what happened to the slaves he captured.

STRATEGY 4:

Literature Circles

Literature Circles, a reading comprehension approach developed by Harvey Daniels, are small temporary discussion groups consisting of students who have chosen to read the same work of literature. Each member of the circle takes on specific responsibilities during the book discussions. The circles meet regularly, and the discussion roles change at each meeting. When the circle finishes a book, the members decide on a way to showcase their literary work for the rest of the class.

Step-by-Step

1. Teacher establishes literature circles consisting of five students each. He makes sure to provide several texts for students to choose from (see storyboard #1).
2. Students in the circle select a book.
3. Teacher introduces students to different roles by creating a poster and student cue cards. The roles include (see storyboards #4-8):
   a. **Artist** – uses some form of artwork or graphic organizer to represent a significant scene or idea from the reading.
   b. **Luminary** – summarizes the important ideas in the passage.
   c. **Director** – writes questions that will lead to discussion by the group.
   d. **Connector** – finds connections between the reading materials and personal experience, a topic studied or a different work of literature.
   e. **Wizard** – discusses words or phrases in the text that are unusual, interesting, or difficult to understand.
4. Teacher assigns each student to one of five roles. Student roles must change each time the group meets, so the teacher needs a system to ensure that students are consistently taking on different roles.
5. When *Literature Circles* are initially formed, the teacher provides extensive feedback and coaching (see storyboard #3).
6. To coach students on their roles, the teacher develops cue cards for what the student with each particular role should contribute to the group (see storyboards #4-8).
7. As groups become more adept at managing conversations on their own, the teacher slowly withdraws his support and facilitates discussion (see storyboard #9).
8. Upon completing a book, the group develops a presentation, project, report, etc. to showcase their literary work.

Literature Circles

1

Have you ever heard of Oprah's book club? Well, before Oprah started her book club on TV, she would invite friends over to her house to discuss books. Now, there wasn't a teacher to talk about the books with Oprah and her friends. Instead, each person in the club needed to ask questions, talk about what happened, and discuss what they found interesting.

2

This year, when you read books, we are going to have book clubs. And, like Oprah and her friends, you are going to discuss books and talk about their messages, themes, and meanings. Our book clubs are called *Literature Circles* and there are going to be five members in each circle who read and discuss books together.

3

The fun thing about *Literature Circles* is that each member of the circle has a role, and every time the circle meets the roles change. From our other reading comprehension strategies, we know a lot about what good readers do when they read. Let's review these strategies and link them to the roles in *Literature Circles*.

What Good Readers Do		Literature Circle Roles
Ask Questions	→	Director
Summarize	→	Luminary
Visualize Ideas	→	Artist
Make Connections	→	Connector
Clarify Words	→	Wizard

Literature Circles

4

When you meet in your *Literature Circle*, the first thing you'll get is your role for that day. Every member is going to get a card, like this, to remind him or her of the role and what to do. Each role requires some writing, so please bring your pencils. Before we get started, let's briefly review the cards for each role.

Director

Generates and asks questions. Make sure the questions get "big" answers that will cause the other students in your group to think carefully about what they read. YOUR JOB IS TO WRITE FOUR QUESTIONS FOR THE PASSAGE. Some ideas for questions are:

* Was there anything in this part of the story that bothered or surprised you?
* If you could talk to the main character, what would you tell him or her to do?
* Do you agree with the main character's actions? Why or why not?
* What do you think will happen in the next part of the story?

1. ______________________________
2. ______________________________
3. ______________________________
4. ______________________________

5

Here is the card that describes what the Luminary does.

Luminary

Your job is to tell the main things that happened in today's reading. To help you make sure that you just focus on the important events, you get only three sentences to summarize what you read.

____

____

____

____

____

Literature Circles

6

The Artist can draw a picture, graphic organizer, comic strip, or any visual that shows a main part of the selection.

Artist

The artist draws a picture or graphic organizer to show a main part of the selection that you read. You can use a sketch, cartoon, chart, or scene. DO NOT COPY DRAWINGS FROM THE BOOK!

What my picture shows: ____________________

Why I chose this event to illustrate: ____________________

7

Let's review the Connector's responsibilities.

Connector

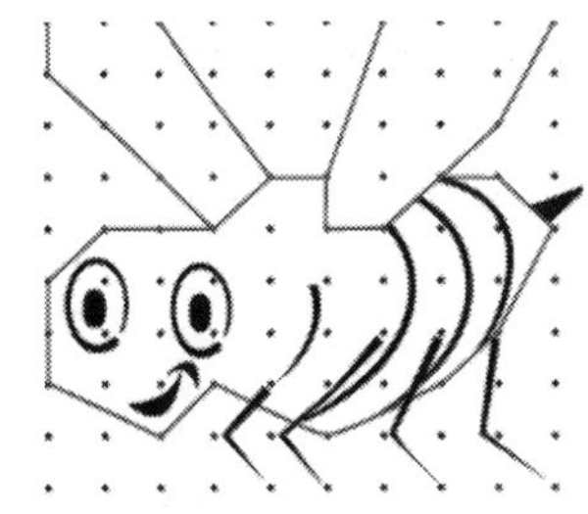

Your job is to write three ways how the selection you are reading connects with

- another book
- an event you saw on the Internet, TV, newspaper.
- your own life

1. ____________________

2. ____________________

3. ____________________

Literature Circles

8

Finally, we have the Wizard card.

Wizard

Your job is to find difficult, puzzling, or unfamiliar words or expressions. Record the page number where you found the word. Then, after reading, find the word in the dictionary, and write down the meaning.

Word **Page** **Dictionary Definition**

1. ____________ Page: ___ Definition: ______________________________

2. ____________ Page: ___ Definition: ______________________________

3. ____________ Page: ___ Definition: ______________________________

4. ____________ Page: ___ Definition: ______________________________

5. ____________ Page: ___ Definition: ______________________________

7

I am going to spend time with each *Literature Circle* and help and coach you with these roles. The point of *Literature Circles* is for your groups to have meaningful discussions about books. So you want to be talking with each other and doing a good job with your role so that everyone in the circle benefits.

References

Buehl, D. (2001). *Classroom strategies for interactive learning*. Second edition. International Reading Association, Newark, DE.

Daniels, H. (2002). *Literature circles: Voice and choice in the student-centered classroom*. Stenhouse Publisher, Portland, ME.

Englert, C.S. & Mariage, T.V. (1991). Making students partners in the comprehension process: Organizing the reading POSSE. *Learning Disabilities Quarterly, 14*, 123-138.

Stahl, K. A., Dougherty, E.. & McKenna, M. C. (2006). *Reading research at work: Foundations of effective practice*. Guilford Publications, New York, NY.

Teaching for Expert Comprehension

8

Throughout this book, we've presented research-proven reading comprehension strategies that increase student achievement 15 to 100 percent. Almost all of these strategies were developed based on what expert readers do to comprehend text.

Picasso's paintings were influenced by artists like de Toulouse-Lautrec and El Greco. Frank Lloyd Wright credits his apprenticeship with Louis Sullivan and his study of Japanese architecture for inspiring his master designs. And, James Patterson, author of 18 international best selling novels, cites Jean Genet as the writer he emulates most. If great painters, architects and writers carefully study and integrate what other experts in their fields do, why shouldn't readers?

But knowing how expert readers think is only half the battle. Transforming that knowledge into instructional strategies is what makes skilled teachers' students shine.

How Master Teachers Teach Comprehension

The visual storyboard examples and 15 DVD videos of master teachers reinforce how researchers recommend teaching reading comprehension. In virtually every instance the teacher:

1. Explicitly introduces the strategy.
2. Shows students how to use the strategy by reading a portion of the text, then thinking aloud and modeling it.
3. Requires students to practice the strategy under teacher supervision.
4. Provides specific feedback and opportunities for students to use the strategy with a variety of texts.
5. Cues students to use the strategy when they encounter new situations.

Not surprisingly, Professors Michael Pressley, Barak Rosenshine, and Nathaniel Gage have all published experimental research demonstrating the effectiveness of this five part strategy instructional approach. Thus, while the reading comprehension strategies explained throughout this book differed, these five instructional recommendations were present in each lesson.

Invest in Comprehension Strategy Instruction

The benefits of teaching students expert comprehension strategies are additive. Research shows that when children are taught just one of the comprehension strategies introduced in this book their reading improves. When students have internalized repertoires of strategies, comprehension grows exponentially.

Over the last thirty years researchers have uncovered expert readers' thinking. Scholars not only defined this strategic thinking, but also developed a wide variety of instructional strategies based on it. Researchers then conducted experimental studies to prove that teaching students expert comprehension strategies increased their reading achievement. Moreover, recent research confirms that students who use many comprehension strategies outperform students who use one or none.

It is our hope that teaching your students a wide variety of scientifically proven reading comprehension strategies will not only dramatically increase their understanding of what they read, but also add color and variety to your literacy instruction.

References

Gage, N. L. & Needels, M. C. (1989). Process-product research on teaching: A review of criticisms. *Elementary School Journal, 89,* 253-300.

Pressley, M. & Wharton-McDonald, R. (1997). Skilled comprehension and its development through instruction. *School Psychology Review, 26*, 279-304.

Rosenshine, B. (1995). Advances in research on instruction. *Journal of Educational Research, 88,* 262-268.

About the Author

John Schacter earned his doctorate from UCLA in educational psychology and graduated with highest honors in Literature from UC San Diego. Before starting *The Teaching Doctors*, Dr. Schacter served as vice president of research for the Milken Family Foundation, Senior Fellow at Stanford's Educational Leadership Institute, and taught educational psychology at San Jose State University.

Dr. Schacter has been invited to testify to numerous state legislatures. He has appeared on National Public Radio, NBC News, and Radio Disney. John's research has been cited in USA Today, The Washington Post, The Baltimore Sun, The Orlando Sentinel and other newspapers and magazines across the country. He has published over 40 research articles and is the author of two books.

If you are interested in information regarding seminars or scheduling professional development for your school visit: **www.teachingdoctors.com** or contact Dr. Schacter directly at **schacter@teachingdoctors.com**.